LAW
AND SOCIAL
CHANGE

Edited by

Stuart S. Nagel

 SAGE PUBLICATIONS *Beverly Hills / London*

K
376
.N3

PUBLISHER'S NOTE:

The material in this publication originally appeared as a special issue of AMERICAN BEHAVIORAL SCIENTIST (Volume 13, Number 4, March/April 1970). The Publisher would like to acknowledge the assistance of the special issue editor, Stuart S. Nagel, in making this edition possible.

For information address:

SAGE PUBLICATIONS, INC.
275 South Beverly Drive
Beverly Hills, California 90212

SAGE PUBLICATIONS LTD
St George's House / 44 Hatton Garden
London EC1N 8ER

Printed in the United States of America

International Standard Book Number 0-8039-0334-0

Library of Congress Catalog Card No. 73-89941

FIRST PRINTING (this edition)

CONTENTS

LAW AND SOCIAL CHANGE

Overview of Law and Social Change

STUART S. NAGEL
University of Illinois

THE BIGGER PICTURE INTO WHICH THIS SYMPOSIUM FITS

In recent years there has been a great increase in legal research in which law is viewed as the response of lawmakers to prior stimuli and also as stimuli to subsequent responses of law appliers and law recipients. Two excellent collections of recent materials presenting various aspects of this dual perspective include the readers by Friedman and Macaulay (1969) and the one by Schwartz and Skolnick (1970).[1] Viewing law as both effects and causes is contrasted with viewing law merely as a set of rules and decisions to be read by students, applied by lawyers, and reacted to as being good or bad by professors. Regardless of one's viewpoint, law can be defined as the rules or decisions made by governmental agencies with regard to how people are supposed to behave particularly with regard to each other.

There are many stimuli or causes that can produce legal policies and adjudications. These include:

(1) broad legal or normative principles from which more narrow legal conclusions can be deduced given certain case facts;

(2) interest group pressures; and

(3) values of the legislators and adjudicators.

One particularly important causal variable is the role of social change. It is particularly important because it tends to shape the broader normative principles, the relative power of interest groups, and the values of policy-makers. Social change refers in this context to a restructuring of the basic ways in which people in a society relate to each other with regard to economics, government, education, religion, family life, recreation, language, and other basic human interaction activities. Although social change is important, changes with regard to technology, science, and demography may be even more fundamental determinants of both social and legal change.

On the impact side of the dual conceptual scheme, there are many responses or effects that can be produced by legal policies and adjudications. These include:

(1) compliance patterns as measured by the extent of law violations;

(2) psychological attitudinal changes; and

(3) behavioral changes other than compliance patterns, such as movement by blacks in response to an open housing law.

These responses can be made by intermediate law appliers or by the ultimate law recipients, and they can be goal responses or side effects. A particularly important effect variable is social change. It is important because by definition, when law produces social change, there has been a basic restructuring of how people in a society relate to each other with regard to basic human interaction activities.

THE CONTENTS OF THIS SYMPOSIUM

It is the purpose of this symposium to discuss:

(1) How can one measure relations between law and social change?

(2) How and when does social change produce legal change?

(3) How and when does legal change produce social change?

(4) How do both forms of change reciprocally interact?

As such it is hoped that this symposium will add to the growing literature which explicitly deals with law and social change in general (Stone, 1965: 119-163; Schur, 1968: 107-141), with a sociological history of law (Friedmann, 1964; Hurst, 1950), or with law as an instrument of social change (Becker, 1969; Mayo and Jones, 1964).

With regard to measuring relations between law and social change, Donald Campbell has been in the forefront of such methodological research (see Campbell, 1968; 1969). In this symposium he joins with Laurence Ross and Gene Glass to produce an article which dovetails well with his earlier (1968) article on the Connecticut speed law crackdown. In that earlier article, the legal change was found to have no valid causal relation with a reduction in auto accident death rates. The criteria of validity used are difficult to meet with regard to eliminating alternative causal variables. In the present article on the British drunk driving crackdown, however, the same criteria were elegantly satisfied. It is hoped that future researchers will apply this quasi-experimental approach to a variety of law and social change situations.

Social change as a force promoting legal change can be viewed in at least two ways. One perspective is to think in terms of law in general, as Thomas Dienes does in his article, and a contrasting perspective is to think in terms of a specific field of law, such as criminal law, as C. Ray Jeffery does in his article. Dienes provides a general conceptual scheme describing the relation between the changing social environment and the responses of interacting legislators and judges. The richness of his sophisticated scheme provides a sharp contrast to the traditional formal textbook approach to the lawmaking process. Jeffery describes the historical social forces responsible for moving criminal law from punishment to deterrence to rehabilitation. He also describes the contemporary social forces responsible for making individual rehabilitation and indirect anti-poverty programs ineffective in reducing crime. He recommends a program of crime control mainly through direct environmental engineering which will substantially reduce the opportunity to commit criminal acts.

Legal change as a force promoting social change can also be viewed in at least two ways. One perspective is value-free, where the researcher is simply concerned with describing the effects of law on behavior and attitudes, as is done in Joel Grossman's article. The other perspective is goal-oriented, where the researcher takes certain goals as given and then describes what policies will optimize or satisfy the goals, as is done in Yehezkel Dror's article. Both approaches are objective in the sense that the researcher's personal values should not significantly influence his perceptions, and his policy evaluations should generally be made only in terms of empirically tested means-ends statements. Grossman is especially concerned with describing variables that determine the Supreme Court's influence, and Dror emphasizes that (1) changing the law is only one of many changes in the total legal system that can bring about social change, and (2) systematic policy science research is needed in order to optimize legal changes. The Levine-Becker article combines Grossman's concern for describing variables that influence Supreme Court impact and Dror's concern for optimizing legal policy.

The final section of the symposium relates to reciprocal relations between law and social change. Marxist theory has long dealt with this reciprocity. On the one hand, law is part of the superstructure that is determined by the economic base of a society. Thus if one knows the extent to which ownership of the means of production and distribution is private rather than collective, and if one knows the extent to which income and wealth is unequally distributed, then one can possibly make many accurate predictions as to what the law will generally provide with regard to how people are supposed to relate to each other in various basic activities. On the other hand, Marxism believes that law is an important instrument for manipulating economic and other social institutions. It is this impact of law on the economy which John Hazard emphasizes in his article, "Law and Social Change in Marxist Africa." One can, however, readily see in the article how the current law of the African countries described has been influenced by their present low-technology economies and by their previous exploitative colonial economies. The final article by Arthur Miller describes six interaction patterns between scientific and legal change, and it ends with a call for law schools and lawyers to meet the challenges of social change brought on by science and technology.

INTEGRATING SOCIAL ROLES AND LEGAL CHANGES

In tying some of these law and social change ideas together, it might be helpful to take about a half-dozen of the most important and most dynamic social roles that people have in the United States to see (1) what impact legal change has had on these changing roles, and (2) what impact these changing roles have had on changes in the law. I think such an analysis will show that in an increasingly highly urbanized and industrialized society like the United States, legal change does play a large part in social change and vice versa, at least much more so than is the case in traditional societies or in traditional sociological thinking.

Perhaps the seven most important social roles of the average American, in somewhat random order, are the roles involved in being a: (1) consumer, (2) family member, (3) citizen, (4) employee, (5) personal property owner, (6) tenant, and (7) an ethnic group member. Over the last fifty years all of these roles have changed tremendously, and the changes have caused legal changes which, in turn, have caused further social changes in a never-ending cycle. Take the *buyer*-seller relationship for instance. Along with increased urbanization and industrialization, the face-to-face relation between the ultimate consumer and the maker of a product or even the owner of the sales outlet has almost ceased to exist. This social change has necessitated more formal legal controls over the quality of products sold and, in some industries, over the prices as well. These legal changes have in turn resulted in changes in the behavior of sellers toward buyers with regard to various deceptive and dangerous practices.

Likewise in the realm of intra*family* relations, urbanization, with its small apartments, has lessened the desirability of three-generation families in a single household. This social change helped cause the establishment of social security laws, which in turn helped generate changes in the labor force and in social institutions for the aged. With regard to the role of the *citizen* vis-à-vis his government, studies have been made, for example, of the social forces responsible for progressive income tax laws, as well as the impact that income tax laws have had on incentives and disincentives to work.

In the field of employer-*employee* relations, much of American labor history prior to the 1930s pointed toward the enactment of precedents and statutes guaranteeing the right to unionize, and once the Wagner Act was passed, the percentage of the labor force in unions did drastically increase although it has since reached a plateau. Because of technological change, the relation of personal property *owners* to other persons has become more impersonal and frequently more likely to lead to injury, and, as a result, there has been a lessening of the legal theory of fault, which in turn has changed the American insurance system.

More recently, interaction between the *races* has resulted in extensive civil rights precedents and legislation which recent studies show have produced significant social changes—although perhaps not significant enough. Change in landlord-*tenant* relations are now necessitating changes in housing codes, which in turn change the tenancy relation. Indeed, all basic interaction roles have changed substantially in the United States in fairly recent years partly because of legal changes which social changes have brought about.

Not all legal change, however, results in social change, since many rules and decisions affect very few people. Likewise, not all social change results in legal change, since some aspects of human interaction in many societies are not covered by formal legal rules, although social change, being more fundamental, is more likely to produce legal change than vice versa. Nevertheless, in spite of frequent nonreciprocal causation, one can say on the basis of the above brief analysis that all major social roles in American life have changed substantially in recent years, and these changes in roles have helped generate changes in some laws, which in turn have produced important social changes.

One particularly interesting development with regard to law as a reciprocal factor in social change is the current involvement of the federal government in a program for deliberately encouraging legal changes in each of the seven basic social roles previously mentioned. The guidelines of the OEO legal services agencies which have sprung up throughout the country explicitly direct the attorneys involved to seek to establish precedents and legislation designed to strengthen the rights of consumers, family members, citizens vis-à-vis government officials, employees, tenants, and minority ethnic group members. The social engineering activities of these legal services agencies should provide a fruitful set of laboratories for studying law as an instrument of social change.

As a further source of potential quantitative data on the role of law in social change, perhaps more before-and-after reseach can be done on the work products of three other organizations that influence much legislation and judicial decisions in all fifty states, namely the Commissioners of Uniform State Laws, the American Law Institute, and the Committee on Suggested State Legislation of the Council of State Governments. These organizations would welcome a more systematic comparative analysis of the impact of the adoption and nonadoption of legislation they have proposed. To carry out some of these grand research schemes, perhaps what is needed is an interuniversity consortium for sociolegal research analogous to the Inter-University Consortium for Political Research operating out of the University of Michigan.

The kind of research proposed should be capable of testing numerous hypotheses about the effects of diverse legislation on behavior and attitudes and also hypotheses about the factors that facilitate or inhibit the impact of such legislation. For lack of methodological skills, this kind of empirical research has tended to be neglected in the law schools; and for lack of substantive interest, it has tended to be neglected in the sociology departments. Perhaps political scientists can help fill the gap. There surely is a need for more theorizing like that represented in most of the articles in this symposium. Perhaps what is needed at least as much is more hard data from such sources as questionnaires, aggregate statistics, and content analysis that can serve as the basis from which inductive generalizations can be drawn, thereby helping to build a behavioral science of law.

NOTE

1. This two-sided perspective of viewing law as both an independent and a dependent variable is also used in Sigler (1968) and Nagel (1969).

REFERENCES

BECKER, T. [ed.] (1969) The Impact of Supreme Court Decisions. New York: Oxford Univ. Press.

CAMPBELL, D. (1969) "Reforms as experiments." Amer. Psychologist 24: 409-429.

--- and L. ROSS (1968) "The Connecticut crackdown on speeding: time-series data in quasi-experimental analysis." Law and Society Rev. 3 (August): 33-53.

FRIEDMAN, L. and S. MACAULAY (1969) Law and the Behavioral Sciences. Indianapolis: Bobbs-Merrill.

FRIEDMANN, W. (1964) Law in a Changing Society. New York: Penguin.

HURST, J. (1950) The Growth of American Law: The Law Makers. Boston: Little, Brown.

MAYO, L. and E. JONES (1964) "Legal policy decision process: alternative thinking and the predictive function." George Washington Law Rev. 33: 318-456.

NAGEL, S. (1969) The Legal Process from a Behavioral Perspective. Homewood, Ill.: Dorsey.

SCHUR, E. (1968) Law and Society: A Sociological View. New York: Random House.

SCHWARTZ, R. and J. SKOLNICK (1970) Society and the Legal Order. New York: Basic Books.

SIGLER, J. (1968) An Introduction to the Legal System. Homewood, Ill.: Dorsey.

STONE, J. (1965) Social Dimensions of Law and Justice. Stanford: Stanford Univ. Press.

Determining the Social Effects of a Legal Reform

The British "Breathalyser" Crackdown of 1967

H. LAURENCE ROSS
University of Denver

DONALD T. CAMPBELL
Northwestern University

GENE V GLASS
University of Colorado

The social effects of a legal reform are examined in this paper utilizing the Interrupted Time-Series research design, a method of analysis that has broad potential use in studies of legal change more generally. A previous demonstration of the applicability of this design to the sociology of law concerned the Connecticut crackdown on speeders (see Campbell and Ross, 1968; Glass, 1968). In that study, the substantive findings were that the crackdown had little effect on the highway death rate, and that it introduced certain unexpected and undesirable changes into the legal process in Connecticut. The present study concerns a similar attempt to lower the highway death rate through changes in the law, specifically the British Road Safety Act of 1967. Critical scrutiny of the data indicates that in this instance the legal change quite impressively achieved its goal.

The British crackdown attempted to get drunken drivers off the road, and thus took aim at a scientifically demonstrated correlate of automobile accidents. The Connecticut crackdown, in contrast, was based on commonsense considerations unsupported even by correlational studies. Its sponsors claimed success prematurely, before such possibilities as random variation and statistical regression could be ruled out as explanations of an apparently striking decline in accident rate. In the present study, similar claims turned out to be justified.

Authors' Note: *This study was supported in part by National Science Foundation Grant G51309X.*

[15]

In presenting this report, we hope for two consequences. Substantively, we hope that officials concerned with traffic safety will consider adopting a legal reform which has proved in one notable instance to be effective in reducing traffic deaths; methodologically, we hope to increase awareness of the need for hard-headed evaluation of legal and administrative reforms, and of the value of experimental and quasi-experimental designs for this purpose.

INTERRUPTED TIME-SERIES ANALYSIS

The Interrupted Time-Series is a quasi-experimental design (Campbell and Stanley, 1966; Campbell, 1969) for studying the effect of a given "treatment" on a variable that is repeatedly measured over a period of time before and after the application of the treatment. Like all quasi-experimental techniques, the time-series design is a substitute for an unfeasible true experiment. The true experiment requires randomized assignments of subjects to experimental and control groups, but the time-series design can be used, albeit with greater equivocality, in situations lacking randomization.

The essence of an Interrupted Time-Series design is the extension of a typical before-and-after study to a series of observations at various times removed from the experimental treatment, both before and after. To illustrate, the typical before-and-after study concerns only points immediately prior and subsequent to the treatment, as in Figure 1, which compares accidental deaths in Connecticut before and after the crackdown on speeding. It is very difficult to interpret any change from before to after the treatment for various reasons, discussed in more detail in our full presentations. Briefly, these reasons are:

(1) History. The change observed may be due to simultaneous events other than the experimental treatment.

(2) Maturation. The change may be part of some long-term trend.

(3) Instrumentation. The measured change may be based on a change in the means of measuring, rather than in the thing being measured.

(4) Testing. The change may be caused by the initial measurement rather than by the treatment.

(5) Instability. The apparent change may be no more than chance or random variation.

(6) Regression. If the group was selected because it was extreme on some measure, statistical reasoning indicates that it will appear less extreme on subsequent tests, even though the intervening treatment may be completely ineffectual.

A study of Figures 1 and 2 of Campbell and Ross (1968: 38, 42) will illustrate the relevance of time-series data to four of these six threats to validity. In this Connecticut case, maturation and testing are pretty well ruled out by the extended data series inasmuch as *both* posit processes that would have existed in prior years and inasmuch as the 1955-1956 drop is not interpretable as a continuation of trends manifest in 1951-1955. History and instrumentation are not controlled by this design, but an examination of plausible alternative causes such as winter weather and possible changes in record-keeping make this implausible as rival explanations of the 1955-1956 drop. It is on the threats of instability and regression that the time-series presentation exposes weaknesses invalidating the public pronouncements on the Connecticut experiment.

Instability was a possibility totally neglected. *All* of the 1955-1956 change was attributed to the crackdown, the Governor of Connecticut stating, "With a saving of forty lives in 1956, a reduction of 12.3% from the 1955 motor vehicle death toll, we can say the program is definitely worthwhile." When the prior years are examined it become obvious that the 1955-1956 shift is typical of the usual annual shifts, rather than being exceptionally large. The problem of regression was likewise overlooked. When a treatment is applied because of extremity on some score (e.g., remedial reading courses applied to persons because of their low reading comprehension scores) it is likely that subsequent scores will on the average be less extreme due to statistical regression alone, even if the treatment has had no effect. The problem of regression is not easy to communicate briefly. It will be helpful to think of a time-series that fluctuates completely at random. If one moves along the series, selecting points that are extraordinarily high, on the average subsequent points will be lower, less extreme and closer to the general trend. In the Connecticut case it appears certain that the great 1954-1955 increase instigated the crackdown. Thus the point where the treatment was instigated was selected for its height. Therefore, a good part of the 1955-1956 decrease must be attributed to statistical regression.

Legal change is a subject for which the Interrupted Time-Series design seems eminently suited. True experiments can seldom be performed in the law because all persons receive the treatment at the same time or because, even if only some receive it, legal or practical considerations prevent the necessary randomization. If a policy strikes a legislature or an administrative body as being a good idea, it is adopted wholesale; if it seems unpromising at first glance, it may not be tried at all. Moreover, even when a change is adopted "experimentally," it is seldom applied at random to one group of people and not to another similarly situated group. The experimental change is typically put into full-scale effect for either an arbitrarily limited time or for a single jurisdiction chosen nonrandomly from among many others. The time-series design is appropriate in these circumstances.

The opportunity to work with time-series designs in studies of legal change is enhanced by the fact that there are numerous series of data that are routinely gathered by governmental bureaus and agencies. Examples are general and specific crime rates, institutional commitments, case loads, economic indexes, and accident rates. Because these data are routinely gathered, their measurement is not taken by participants as a cue that a study is being done (Webb et al., 1966). Generalization to other groups involves fewer theoretical problems than for laboratory experiments because of the much greater similarity between field of experimentation and field of application.

The special relevance of time-series data for questions of legal impact has no doubt frequently been recognized, even though simple before-and-after figures, or percentage change from the previous year remain the commonest means of reporting. Time-series data have been employed by Stieber (1949) and Rose (1952) in studies of the effects of compulsory arbitration; by Wolf, Luke and Hax, (1959), Rheinstein (1959) and Glass (1971) in studies of divorce law; and by Walker (1965) and Schuessler (1969) in studies of the effects of capital punishment. But the formal development of the method, the analysis of its strengths and pitfalls, and the development of appropriate tests of significance, are all too recent for method to have received the widespread application it deserves. We have previously reported a negative application, primarily rejecting the Connecticut claims. In the present paper we report an optimistic one, in which effects claimed in press releases stand up under scientific scrutiny.

ALCOHOL AND TRAFFIC ACCIDENTS

THE LEGISLATION AND BACKGROUND

The sponsors of the British Road Safety Act of 1967 based their action on a voluminous scientific literature which showed association between accidents, particularly serious ones, and blood alcohol, particularly in high concentrations. In a recent review of the literature, three studies of fatal accidents were cited in which the proportion of drivers with alcohol in their bloodstreams ranged from 55 to 64%. In single-vehicle accidents, three other studies revealed alcohol in from 71 to 83% of the victims (Automobile Manufacturers Association, 1966). One of the latter studies matched the deceased drivers with a sample obtained later of drivers in the same location at the same hour. Only 23% of the controls had a concentration of .02% or more of alcohol in their blood, compared with 71% of the deceased drivers.

There were similar findings in reports of several correlational studies of nonfatal accidents. The U.S. Department of Transportation recently issued a report containing the following summary:

> Scientific investigation of actual crashes and the circumstances in which they occur and laboratory and field experiments show very clearly that the higher a driver's blood alcohol concentration:
>
> —the disproportionately greater is the likelihood that he will crash;
>
> —the greater is the likelihood that he himself will have initiated any crash in which he is involved; and
>
> —the greater is the likelihood that the crash will have been severe.
>
> [House Committee on Public Works, 1968: 15]

The British government, then, had a good theoretical basis on which to form their program of control. The attempt was further justified by claims of success in similar programs in the Scandinavian countries (Andanaes, 1966). The state of knowledge about alcohol and accidents is quite different from the existing knowledge about the effect of speed, which indicates no simple relationship with accidents.

Since 1925, it had been an offense in Britain to drive while under the influence of alcohol. However, as one British lawyer explained:

> I knew only too well how easy it was to secure acquittal from a charge of drunken driving in the United Kingdom. The form one adopted for the defense was always to insist on a jury trial; the evidence as to drunkenness was always given by the Police Surgeon who had made the drunken man carry out some rather extraordinary tests, many of which perfectly sober people could not carry out. You would inevitably find that your jury consisted of people like myself, honest, law-abiding citizens who both drove motor cars and also drank alcohol. The inevitable reaction of juries faced with a case of this nature was "there but [for] the grace of God go I . . . Not Guilty" [Insurance Institute for Highway Safety, 1968: 40].

Legislation in 1962 permitted blood and urine tests, with certain presumptions to be raised in the event of the driver's refusal to cooperate. The stimulus for additional legislation was a continued rise in automobile-related deaths and serious injuries. Deaths had peaked in 1966 at 7,985, a culmination of a steady rise throughout the 1950s and 1960s. Injuries peaked a year earlier, but remained quite high (384,000) in 1966.

The new legislation, put into effect on October 9, 1967, was not particularly radical as compared, for instance, with Scandinavian procedures, or even with the laws in several American states. However, the Act was well publicized in Britain and included the following features:

(1) The criterion of impairment was set at a blood alcohol level of .08%. This is a more stringent standard than that prevailing in most American states, but less so than that prevailing in Norway and Sweden (.05%) or in Czechoslovakia, Bulgaria, and East Germany (.03%). A blood alcohol level of .08% might be barely reached if a 160-pound man drank three drinks in quick succession on an empty stomach (Campbell, 1964).

(2) Police were authorized to give an on-the-scene breath test. This test, popularly called the breathalyser, gave its name to the crackdown in the British press. The test may be administered to a driver if "the constable has reasonable cause— (a) to suspect him of having alcohol in his body; or (b) to suspect him of having committed a traffic offense while the vehicle was in motion." The test may also be given to any driver involved in an accident. A driver who fails the breath test is brought to the police station for a (more accurate) blood or urine test, on the basis of which a charge is made.

(3) A mandatory punishment was instituted, consisting of "disqualification" (license suspension) for one year and a fine of £100 or imprisonment for up to four months, or both. Severe penalties were also instituted for failure to submit to the breath test or to either the blood or urine tests.

(4) The specific starting date for the new regulations was given advance publicity. This provides an essential aspect making the study interpretable. A very gradual change of enforcement would have produced results indistinguishable from a gradual change in long-term trends.

Although official publicity campaigns greatly increased public awareness of the new procedures and penalities, particularly of the on-the-scene breathalyzer test, enforcement was probably not much increased. During the first six months after the act was initiated, only 20,000 drivers had to take the test, and fewer than half of them failed it. A report commissioned by the Insurance Institute for Highway Safety states "that in reality [the British driver's] chances of being apprehended for driving after drinking are no greater than they were before" (Bennett and Westwick, 1968: 10).

CLAIMED RESULTS

As in the case of the Connecticut crackdown, the fact of fewer casualties in the period immediately following the institution of the reform was interpreted as evidence of an effect. The Ministry of Transport in its official press releases was considerably more restrained than the governor of Connecticut had been, but its claims were based on much the same kind of reasoning. For instance, a press release of March 21, 1968, was headlined: "Road Casualties in 1967 Lowest Figure for Nine Years." This release documented the fact that in the last three months of 1967 casualties had declined by sixteen percent and deaths had declined by twenty-three percent; readers were reminded that the Road Safety Act came into force on the 9th of October. On December 11, 1968, the Ministry of Transport issued a press release headline: "First Twelve Months of 'Breath Test.' 1,152 Fewer Dead on Roads." Although the term "cause" was never used, the report contains statements about "casualty savings" and "gaining safety from the new legislation." The magnitude of the shift, particularly in the night hours when the casualty rate declined by a third, makes the British interpretation less offensive than the official line in Connecticut. Our statistical analyses, in fact, support the press releases. But the claims failed to indicate that thought had been given to such obvious alternative causes of the decline as instability of the casualty rate, regression from peak statistics, and other safety-related events taking place at the same time.

INTERRUPTED TIME-SERIES ANALYSIS
OF THE BREATHALYSER CRACKDOWN

THE STATISTICS

A graphic presentation of some of our time-series analysis of the breathalyser crackdown is shown in Figure 1. Our analyses are based upon statistics made available to us by the British Ministry of Transport, including breakdowns going beyond the data reported in their press releases, some of which were made especially at our request.[1] We report

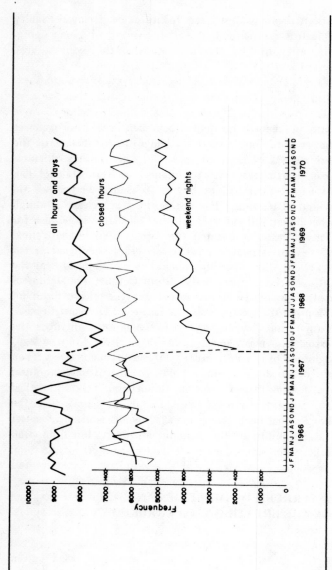

Figure 1.

British traffic casualties (fatalities plus serious injuries) before and after the breathalyser crackdown of October 9, 1967, seasonally adjusted. (Note: This figure is a corrected and extended version of the one in the original printing and is based upon Figures 7, 8, 10, and 11 from H. L. Ross, Law, science, and accidents: The British Road Safety Act of 1967, *The Journal of Legal Studies*, 1973, 2, 1-78 (#1, January), also available in *Research Contributions of the American Bar Foundation*, 1973, No. 1.)

here only a portion of our analyses, selected so as to display the major results and to illustrate the method.

All hours and days. Data on total monthly casualty rates by seriousness of casualty are available back to 1961. For the present analysis, we have focused upon the combination "fatalities plus serious casualties," since specific hour and day analyses, to be discussed later, were only available in that form. These data have been smoothed in two stages: first, the rates for months of 28, 29, and 30 days in length have been extrapolated to 31-day equivalents (by multiplying the obtained rates by 31/28, and so forth). Second, a yearly cycle of seasonal variation has been removed. (In this cycle, January is lowest, August through December high.) The average monthly rate prior to the crackdown has been used to compute a monthly correction such that the mean annual correction is zero. These corrections have been added to, or subtracted from, the 31-day rates. The crackdown began on October 9, 1967. In order to plot October as a purely posttreatment value, an additional prorating has been employed.[2] Without the prorating, October 1967 would have had a plotted value of 7681, instead of 7226 shown.

Visual inspection of the all-hours-and-days graph supports the hypothesis that the crackdown had an effect. A simple nonparametric consideration offers further confirmation: the September-October drop of 1967 is the largest one-month shift not only for the three years plotted in Figure 1, but also for the total series going back to January 1961. The odds against this are 93 to 1. This holds true even if the uncorrected value for October 1967 is used. The most sophisticated test of significance in this situation is that developed by Box and Tiao (1965).[3]

Taking out the annual seasonal cycle is a problematic matter (and even more so in the shorter series that follows). Our procedure is only one of many, all of which are unsatisfactory in one way or another. Can the effect be noted in these all-hours-and-days data without the annual cycle being removed? Only if one compensates for it by eye, or by seasonally controlled comparisons. The largest shifts in the uncorrected data tend to be the annual December-January drops, four out of seven larger than our focal September-October 1967. On the other hand, the 1967 September-October drop of 1,654 (or of 1,199 if October be left with the eight precrackdown days uncorrected for) greatly exceeds the seven other September-October shifts, being three times as large as the largest of them.

Week-end nights. Going back continuously until January 1966, the Ministry of Transport has monthly statistics by hours of the week. From their analyses and press releases, it was apparent that Friday and Saturday nights, from 10:00 P.M. to 4:00 A.M. the following morning, were the hours in which the effect of the Breathalyser was strongest. The bottom time-series in Figure 1 depicts these data. Here, the figures have been prorated to four Fridays and four Saturdays each month. Rather than attempt to estimate seasonal cycles on the basis of these few data, it seemed appropriate to use the monthly corrections based on all hours and days, proportionately reduced in magnitude.

These data provide striking evidence of efficacy. The casualty rate seems to drop initially some forty to forty-five percent, and to level off with a net reduction of perhaps thirty percent.

The September-October 1967 drop is four times as large as any other month-to-month change. The Box and Tiao statistic produces *t* in excess of 6.50 for likely magnitudes of effect, for which the chance probability is less than .0000001.

For these weekend nights, the data are convincing visually even when seasonal corrections are not made. Even then, the 1967 September-October drop far exceeds any other month-to-month change, including the December-January ones.

We have chided the typical administrator for being too quick to announce success without taking into account instability, and without adequate sampling time periods before and after the legal change. But when does the administrator have enough evidence? This is in part a function of the prior instability of the series, and in part a function of the magnitude of the change. In the present instance, using the Box and Tiao test and the common acceptance level of a chance probability of less than .01, the administrator could have announced a significant drop after only one posttreatment month. As a matter of fact, after only one month the *t* value was 8.63 where $p < .01 = 2.86$, $p < .001 = 3.88$. Even for the all-hours-and-days data, he would have had to wait only one month, at which time the *t* value was 3.27.

Commuting hours as a control. While both series of data considered so far indicate that the crackdown had an immediate effect, it becomes important to know to what extent that effect has been sustained. Such considerations involve inferences as to what the long-term trends would have been without the crackdown. On the basis of increased traffic volume, one would expect a steady rise. On the basis of increased availability of divided and limited access highways, one would expect a decline. The trend was actually downward 1961-1963, markedly upward 1963-1965, and slightly downward from January, 1966 until the crackdown. Thus there are no grounds here for extrapolation.

What one needs in such cases is a "control group" or some other control comparison. In the Connecticut case, we were able to use data from adjacent and similar states for this purpose, assuming similar weather, vehicles, and safety changes in the absence of a crackdown. Such comparisons never achieve the effectiveness of the randomly assigned control groups of true experiments, but are nonetheless useful. Because of differences in drinking and closed hours, as well as rate of automobilization and highway construction, Irish or Belgian data would be of less use as a control than were other states for Connecticut, but they would still be of value.

But control data series need not come solely from different persons, groups or populations. In the present situation, a valuable comparison would come from those high accident hours least likely to be affected by drinking. Commuting hours during which British pubs and bars are closed seemed ideal. Casualties on the five working days between the hours of 7:00 to 10:00 A.M. and 4:00 to 5:00 P.M. were chosen (pubs close after lunch at 2:30 P.M.). These monthly rates were prorated to 23 working days per month. These data showed a distinctly different annual cycle than did the all-hours-and-days data; rather than January being the lowest month, August was, whereas August was the highest in the all-hours-and-days cycle. November and December were high in both cycles. These differences made it inappropriate to use the 1961-1967 annual cycle used for the other two curves. Since the commuting-hour data showed much the same cycle each of the three years (except that the high was November rather than December in 1968) and since there was only trivial indication of effect, the three years of these data were averaged to get the annual cycle, which was then removed from the series.

In Figure 1, the middle line represents the resulting commuting-hours series. There is visibly no effect of the crackdown, nor does the Box and Tiao test show one, when applied to the series as graphed, or to an alternate way of removing the annual cycle. (The graphed approach would have some bias in the direction of minimizing the September-October 1967 shift.)

Ideally, this commuting-hour series would provide a control comparison against which we could decide whether or not the Breathalyser enforcement was being maintained or had abated. Insofar as it is relevant for this purpose, the crackdown had a maximum impact for the first three or four months and has leveled off since. But at the end of 1968 there was still a definite saving of some thirty percent in the weekend-night rates.

The appropriateness of the comparison is weakened by the dissimilarity shown in its annual cycle. Yet it is the nearest thing we have. If it is to be of value we need to do better than has been done here with the annual trend. Data subsequent to the crackdown continue to be collected, and four or five years from now we will have available a better estimate of the commuting-hour annual cycle.

THE THREATS TO VALIDITY

In the presentation of the Interrupted Time-Series design at the beginning of this paper, we listed six threats to validity. In the presentation so far of the British crackdown, we have paid attention primarily to the threat of instability—the only one, it should be remembered, to which tests of significance are relevant.

Reviewing the other threats, *maturation* seems out: the October 1967 drop is not plausibly interpretable as part of a general trend manifested prior to the crackdown. *Testing* and *instrumentation* seem unlikely: the procedures for recording and publicizing traffic casualties were well established prior to the crackdown and did not change on account of the crackdown. But this is not a trivial matter. The official categories of "seriously injured" and "slightly injured" obviously call for a judgment the threshold for which could change if the record-keepers were strongly motivated to make a good show. Crime rates, for example, have shown such fluctuations (Etzioni, 1968; Campbell, 1969: 415). In this regard it is comforting to note that for the all-days-and-hours figures, for which fatalities are separately available, they show as marked effects as do serious injuries. (In the crime studies cited, homicides and murders were markedly less susceptible to recording bias than were lesser crimes. See Campbell, 1969.) *Regression* seems implausible here, for, in marked contrast to the Connecticut case, the crackdown was not a reaction to a peak crisis, but rather to a chronic condition, as inspection of the series indicates.

There remains the catchall category labeled *history*—discrete events other than the experimental treatment that occurs simultaneously with them. In quasi-experimental thinking, when a set of hypotheses cannot be ruled out mechanically through design, the researcher bears the burden of seeking out the reasonable hypotheses included therein and ruling them out or allowing for them individually. The following explanations have been suggested as possible alternative or additional explanations of the change in the British casualty rate in October of 1967 (Bennett and Westwick, 1968).

(1) *The publicizing of crackdown.* The government conducted a two-phase publicity campaign concerning the crackdown, from September 25 through December 21, 1967. This large-scale effort involved several hundred thousand pounds spent for paid advertising, in addition to donations of large amounts of free time by public radio and television. The campaign publicized and explained the crackdown.

Although the publicity campaign may have helped the crackdown produce its effect—indeed, it may be considered as a part of the crackdown—the continued lower casualty rate is inconsistent with the idea that the publicity campaign acted independently. It seems reasonable to posit that the publicity campaign made the crackdown more effective, and to expect that the effect of the crackdown might be increased with additional publicity campaigns. An additional reason for doubting the independent effect of the publicity campaign is the known ineffectiveness of most safety publicity; a similar safety campaign conducted in Britain in 1964, on the same scale and with the same media as the 1967 campaign, had no notable effect on the casualty rate.

(2) *Improvements in traffic controls.* Within the past two or three years, there have been some important improvements in traffic control in Britain. For instance, the priority of vehicles at traffic circles has been resolved, and signs posted accordingly; "halt" and "yield" signs had been posted to control entry to major arteries; and intersections known to be dangerous had been reworked.

Perhaps part of the observed change in the casualty rate is due to these efforts, but the introduction of reforms in traffic control can best be conceived as a gradual program rather than as a sudden one, whereas the change in the data is abrupt. In addition, traffic signs would not be expected to have a greater effect at night than during the day.

(3) *Tire inspection.* New tires must now meet the standards of the British Standards Association. However, since the proportion of vehicles with new tires increases very gradually, the comments concerning the traffic control program apply here and rule out explaining much of the observed change in these terms.

(4) *Reduction in two-wheeled vehicles.* Motorcycles and motor scooters have a high accident rate; the number of these vehicles in use is alleged to have decreased very sharply in 1967, one estimate being as much as thirty percent (Bennett and Westwick, 1968). The reduction is said to be due to a temporary increase in the purchase tax on these vehicles, which was rescinded in 1968.

The factual basis of this explanation is challenged by statistics maintained by the Ministry of Transport showing that the use of motorcycles and motor scooters declined only about fourteen percent in 1967. This decline was part of a general, long-term decline in the use of these vehicles, and was about average in amount. A decline of this form is unlikely to produce an abrupt effect in a causally related variable. Just to be sure, we have examined all-hours-and-days figures separately for cars and for two-wheeled motor vehicles. The sharp October 1967 drop exists in both series, but is much more marked for four-wheeled cars.

(5) *Improvement in traffic law enforcement in London* has been suggested as a cause of the decline.

Since there is no demonstrated sharp and direct relationship between law enforcement and accident rates, this explanation can be discounted.

(6) *Highway traffic* has grown less rapidly in Britain since 1965 than before that date.

However, since growth has continued, albeit at a slower pace, an absolute decrease in the number of accidents does not seem reasonably explained by this fact. The actual volume of traffic in Britain increased by six percent in 1967.

(7) *British insurance companies* offer an enormous discount for claim-free driving.

This is no innovation, and any effect that it might have on casualties would not be expected to follow the form of our data.

CONCLUSION

The Interrupted Time-Series design used in this study of the British crackdown on drinking and driving has ruled out a wide variety of potential alternative explanations of the observed decline in casualties. The only serious contenders to the hypothesis that the crackdown saved lives and injuries are a group of hypotheses each of which refers to a simultaneous event that might be expected to have a similar effect. However, close attention to each of these rules them out as plausible explanations of much of the change observed at the time of the crackdown. Our conclusion is that the crackdown, with its attendant publicity, did save lives and prevent injuries, and that it continues to have an important beneficial effect on British highways.

Substantively, we have shown that a relatively simple and inexpensive legal reform has produced the results for which it was intended. We believe that the British Act, with appropriate modifications, would meet the requirements of constitutionality in the United States; and although direct generalization is not possible, we can see no reasons why such action would not have a similarly beneficial effect in this country. Officials charged with responsibility for highway safety might well be urged to consider this adoption.

Methodologically, we have demonstrated a technique for evaluating the effect of social changes generally and legal changes in particular. This technique ought to be used more frequently than it is at present by both pure and applied social research. The student of society does not need experimental control to assess the effect of a change, providing he knows the limits of the techniques he uses and proceeds sensibly rather than mechanically. If the resulting knowledge is imperfect, the same problem applies in a slightly lesser degree to the best controlled laboratory experiments when one tries to generalize beyond the laboratory. In contrast, the ability to generalize to a large population outside the laboratory is inherent in this and other quasi-experimental techniques where the basic experiment itself is conducted in a similar field situation. Uniquenesses in such settings make it of course desirable to have replications and cross-validations.

The administrator who wants to adopt an innovation such as this should introduce it in such a way that its effectiveness can be reconfirmed in his own setting. For this purpose, where the Interrupted Time/Series is all that is feasible, rules should be kept in mind. First, an abrupt, strong, dateable point of impact should be sought, since gradual innovation cannot be distinguished from secular trends. Second, the available time-series records should be continued so as to preserve comparability. Third, the innovation should be introduced when the problem is at a chronic level, rather than in response to crisis. Fourth, the administrator should seek out control series, from adjacent political units or from subset data within his own polity.

NOTES

1. For these data, we are indebted to N. F. Digance and J. M. Munden, Directorate of Statistics, Ministry of Transport, London. Their help is gratefully

acknowledged.

2. This prorating procedure assumed that the rate for the first nine days of October 1967 was characteristic of October 1961-1966 and of the year 1967. The average October value was 9042. January-September of 1967 ran 1.058 times the average January-September 1.058 x 9042 = anticipated October 1967 of 9566, 8/31 of which is 2468. The actual total for October 1967 was 8269, of which we assume that 8269 - 2468 = 5801 occurred during October 9 to 31. Expanding 5801 for 23 days to a 31-day month produces 7814. (This is then corrected for seasonal trend by subtracting 588, to achieve the plotted point of 7226.) It is obvious here, in the monthly prorating to 31 days, and in the prorating of weekends below, that for a scientific or legislatively authoritative analysis, we should have been given access to records by days rather than by months. However, this was not feasible.

3. Their model assumes that the time/series is subjected to an influence at each time which tends to move the series up or down, and that in the long run these influences—if they could be examined individually—would follow a normal distribution. Though a new influence enters maximally at each point, the effect of the influence is felt on the series at points beyond its initial appearance. Thus the statistical model specifically takes into account the nonindependence of adjacent observations in a time-series. It is with respect to this typical nonindependence of real data that attempts to solve the problems of time-series analysis with simple regression models fail. Data which conform to the statistical model will not show regular periodic cycles. Since most systems which are partially affected by weather and other annual phenomena show yearly cycles, it is necessary to remove such cycles in the data before analysis. Subsidiary autocorrelation analyses verify the absence of cycles. Glass, Tiao, and Maguire (1970) have modified the model to allow for the data to show constant rates of "drift," increase or decrease, over time. It is this modified model which has been used here, applied to the total series, beginning January 1961. For all the likely values of the effect, the t values are 4.0 or larger, which indicates that the shift is of a magnitude that would occur by chance less than once in 10,000 similar series.

REFERENCES

ANDANAES, J. (1966) "The general preventive effects of punishment." Univ. of Pennsylvania Law Rev. 114 (March): 949-983.
Automobile Manufacturers Association, Inc. (1966) The State of the Art of Traffic Safety: A Critical Review and Analysis of the Technical Information on Factors Affecting Traffic Safety. Cambridge: Arthur D. Little.
BENNETT, R. O. and E. H. WESTWICK (1968) "A report on Britain's road safety act of 1967." Prepared for the Insurance Institute of Highway Safety.
BOX, G. E. P. and G. C. TIAO (1965) "A change in level of non-stationary time series." Biometrika 52: 181-192.
CAMPBELL, D. T. (1969) "Reforms as experiments." Amer. Psychologist 24 (April): 409-429.
--- and H. L. ROSS (1968) "The Connecticut crackdown on speeding: time-series data in quasi-experimental analysis." Law & Society Rev. 3 (August): 33-53.

CAMPBELL, D. T. and J. C. STANLEY (1966) Experimental and Quasi-Experimental Designs for Research. Chicago: Rand-McNally.

CAMPBELL, H. E. (1964) "The role of alcohol in fatal traffic 'accidents' and measures needed to solve the problem." Michigan Medicine 63 (October): 699-703.

ETZIONI, A. (1968) "Shortcuts to social change?" The Public Interest 12: 40-51.

GLASS, G. V (1968) "Analysis of the Connecticut speeding crackdown as a time-series quasi-experiment." Law & Society Rev. 3 (August): 55-76.

GLASS, G. V, G. C. TIAO, and T. O. MAGUIRE (1971) "Analysis of data on the 1900 revision of the German divorce laws as a quasi-experiment." Law & Society Rev. 5(May): 539-562.

Insurance Institute for Highway Safety (1968) Highway Safety, Driver Behavior: Cause and Effect. Washington.

RHEINSTEIN, M. (1959) "Divorce and the law in Germany: a review." Amer. J. of Sociology 65: 489-498.

ROSE, A. M. (1952) "Needed research on the mediation of labor disputes." Personnel Psychology 5: 187-200.

ROSS, H. L. (1973) "Law, science, and accidents: the British Road Safety Act of 1967." J. of Legal Studies 2 (January): 1-78.

SCHUESSLER, K. F. (1969) "The deterrent influence of the death penalty," pp. 378-388 in W.J. Chambliss (ed.) Crime and the Legal Process. New York: McGraw-Hill.

STIEBER, J. W. (1949) Ten Years of the Minnesota Labor Relations Act. Minneapolis: Industrial Relations Center, University of Minnesota.

U.S. House Committee on Public Works (1968) 1968 Alcohol and Highway Safety Report. Washington: U.S. Government Printing Office.

WALKER, N. (1965) Crime and Punishment in Britain. Edinburgh: Edinburgh Univ. Press.

WEBB, E. J. et al. (1966) Unobtrusive Measures: Nonreactive Research in the Social Sciences. Chicago: Rand-McNally.

WOLFE, E., G. LÜKE, and H. HAX (1959) Scheidung und Scheidungsrecht: Grudfrägen der Ehescheidung in Deutschland. Tübingen: J.C.B. Mohr.

Judges, Legislators, and Social Change

C. THOMAS DIENES
University of Houston

THE BASIC INTERACTION SCHEME

Through the centuries, men have grappled with the problems posed by their changing environment. In modern society, this task takes on a new sense of urgency as scientific and technological advances occur in a geometric progression. Law and legal institutions play a vital role in this change process by influencing the extent to which interests favoring or opposing change are recognized, encouraged, or impeded. Thus perceived, law is a social institution for achieving desired ends, and a prime consideration in legal analysis must be the capacity of legal institutions to adjust to the changing social environment.

Nor is it sufficient merely to note that a legal system is composed of interacting institutions responding to changing social demands. Understanding must be based on an ability to describe the actual workings of the system in terms of time and change. What is also increasingly needed is an analytic framework which will suggest specific hypotheses for future research on how the system functions and which will also encompass past research and place it in a new perspective. This study is an attempt to indicate some directions for such inquiry.

Legal institutions may be approached as a "system of action" subject to inputs from the social environment in the form of demands of

---

Author's Note: *This article is derived from a more comprehensive study developing and applying the proposed conceptual framework and written in fulfillment of the Ph.D. requirements of Northwestern University, Department of Political Science. A more complete compilation of the sources on which the framework is based can be obtained from that study.*

conflicting interests affected by social change seeking recognition (Auerbach, 1961; Hart and Sacks, 1958). The conversion process consists of the interactive and decisional behavior of the policy-making actors in the system, e.g., legislature and judiciary; the output takes the form of decisions recognizing interests, settling disputes, and allocating values. Feedback occurs through the impact of the legal norms on the social environment and communication of that impact to the lawmaking actors.

These actors are affected not only by pressures generated by their external environment, but also by their orientations towards the other institutions within the system, i.e., an interaction process. Each institution is itself a subsystem composed of interacting individuals, e.g., legislators and judges, whose behavior also results from their orientations towards one another and other actors outside the subsystem. Interaction may take the form of conflict, cooperation, or accommodation. Demand from the social environment is viewed as a disturbance within the legal system which then reacts to the stress. While a severe stress could alter the system or subsystem, a decision which controls it is the more likely result. The initial task, then, is to delineate the conditions under which the legal system is asked to respond to a change situation.[1]

INITIAL LEGAL RESPONSE

THE RECOMMENDING FUNCTION: PROMOTION OF POLICY ALTERNATIVES

It is often argued that there is recourse to public decision-makers only when a conflict generated by change cannot be settled by private social devices, or when an interest seeks public recognition of a private settlement in its favor (Auerbach, 1959: 83; Hart and Sacks, 1958: 721; Selznick, 1963: 83). Under these circumstances, the demand for action may be addressed to any of the legal subsystems—legislature, judiciary, executive, or administrative agencies. However, we actually know very little about the decision to seek legal redress. There is need for both theory and data on the multiple input sources to the legal forums, on the conditions increasing the saliency of a particular forum, and on the strategies available for gaining access. Essentially, this is the communications problem: how are needs produced by changing social conditions communicated to a particular legal actor? Why is this particular legal actor chosen as a forum? These are only suggestive of the questions that must be answered for an evaluation of the recommending process; they are not so much concerned with whether a favorable decision will be secured as with who initiates action, how the action is initiated, and why a particular forum is chosen.

It can be suggested, for example, that legal response as between the legislature and judiciary in a change situation tends initially to be a product of judicial rather than legislative action. *Legislative* response designed to meet a societal problem through a change in legal norms tends to occur:

(a) when there is an organized and articulate interest group seeking change;

(b) when a substantial harm is resulting from inaction and the proposed soultion appears the most practical;

(c) when the perceived political consequences favor taking action;

(d) when the personal value system of the legislator is favorable to action;

(e) when institutional variables, e.g., rules and personal relationships, favor taking action.[2]

An analysis of these factors affecting access to the legislative process suggests that unorganized, inarticulate interests (i.e., individuals in either unorganized or weakly organized groups, or individuals not fully aware of their needs) can provide little impetus for legislative response (e.g., until recently, welfare recipients). Similarly, legislative institutional response to rapid social change arguably tends to lag behind social change partially because the organization needed to obtain even a hearing takes time to develop.

The courts, on the other hand, unlike the legislature, arguably cannot refuse to hear a dispute "because the job is hard, or dubious, or dangerous" (Llewellyn, 1930). The judiciary lacks the legislative prerogative of deciding that a matter has not developed to a point of justifying action, that it must be given a lower priority, that it is politically too hot to handle, or that another branch must act first. In referring a matter to another branch, it denies a claim; refusal to take action regarding the claim, thereafter serving as precedent. Nor can a judge, like the legislator, initiate a policy decision on his own volition; he lacks a self-starter. Further, it is considered bad form for him as contrasted to the parties to define the issues to be adjudicated. Judicial policy action, therefore, is dependent on the ability and willingness of adverse social interests to press their claims in the judicial forum (Jacob, 1965: 506; Murphy, 1964: 21).

As has frequently been noted, however, the courts are particularly attractive to change interest (e.g., civil rights and anti-poverty interests) since access is more readily available. Any individual litigant has standing to press his claim to the courts. But while the judiciary is available to the individual litigant, this does little good if he lacks the means to initiate and press a claim. Court litigation is often a long, drawn-out process and change interests frequently lack the means or inclination to suffer through the requisite ordeal. The increased emphasis being placed on assuring legal representation for the poor can be perceived as an attempt to assure more adequate lines of communication to the legal system for otherwise inarticulate interests.

THE INTELLIGENCE FUNCTION: INFORMING THE POLICY-MAKER

Assuming that the demand has been pressed on the legal system, the question arises as to the capacity of the particular legal actor to process the data necessary for effective social engineering. Social change posits a relatively new social situation for which adequate data might well be quite scarce, suggesting the danger of an information gap. If lawmaking is to be creative, it must be an informed activity.

Some students of decision-making have approached the process as a rational means-end type of action through which needs are established, alternative modes of meeting the problem are defined, a particular goal is selected, and appropriate means prescribed (see Churchman, 1961; Dror, 1968; Simon, 1958). Others picture the decisional process in incremental terms, a more haphazard form of action under "conditions of bounded rationality." There are at best only "successive limited comparisons" of alternative policies, a gradual approximation by the decision-maker toward some ill-defined objective (Lindblom, 1963). Given the pressures produced by a change situation, it seems likely that the incrementalist approach is a more accurate description of policy formation. But whatever the actual mode of decision-making, the purposive approach assumes an attempt to process those facts upon which decisions can be made. It is necessary, therefore, to consider further the fact-gathering capabilities of the individual legal actors.

In the case of the legislature, for example, this means attention to the fact-gathering performance of legislative hearings and floor debate, to the role of interest groups as information conduits, and to the new devices presently being developed to assist the legislature in achieving its potential for truly effective fact-finding, e.g., law revision commissions and research staff and library services.

A judicial counterpart of the legislative hearings is the trial. Unlike the legislative inquiry, however, court proceedings are governed by far more formalized rules and procedures. The task of gathering and presenting information is charged to the adversary parties themselves, reflecting the belief that through their desire for success the requisite data will emerge. However, the decision in the adjudicatory process is rendered in the context of a concrete case which often severely restricts the scope of the inquiry.

Courts, in handling extremely complex sociolegal problems, can only deal with specific facets of the problem as they are presented. Of course, the language of an opinion can anticipate questions and provide rather substantial clues as to their disposition, but these are tangential to the inquiry and fall under that nebulous classification of dictum. Even if the courts over time could, through case-by-case decision, fashion a comprehensive policy, the rate of change in modern society challenges the adequacy of this process and archaic rules and judges' inhibitions often prevent the admission of the necessary data. This alleged information preeminence of the legislature has frequently led judges to advocate deference to legislative judgment and is often cited as a primary obstacle to effective creative judicial policy action.

THE PRESCRIPTIVE FUNCTION: ENACTING LEGAL NORMS

Finally, in considering the character of the initial legal response to a change situation, it is necessary to consider those factors which influence the final prescriptive behavior of the particular legal actor.

The legislator, for example, must assess the perceived political consequences of a particular action (including constituency pressures, party demands, and interest group activities); he is subjected to the influence of his own personal value system and he must operate under a set of institutional rules of the game. Studies of judicial behavior suggest similar *external forces* also operate on the judicial actor, but that their salience may be markedly different.[3] Whereas the legislator is openly subjected to an array of political pressures, judges aguably tend to be more insulated from direct pressure; external forces tend to operate more indirectly and subliminally. While bargaining may be common in collegial courts, it tends to be more discreet and invisible than in legislative prescriptive behavior (Murphy, 1964). Role orientation regarding the judicial function appears to be a pervasive influence (Becker, 1964).

The salience of external forces may be affected not only by the character of the judicial actor's institutional environment but also by the *circumstances of the decision*. When a new legal problem generated by social change arises, the court is required to act without the traditional guidance supplied by precedent or statute. This is the case of first instance, or the unprovided case, which maximizes the strain on the resources of the courts while affording an excellent opportunity for judicial creativity. What does a judge do when he is required to decide such a dispute? How does he strike a balance between the need for change and the desire to maintain stability and continuity with the past? If he decides to innovate, does he preempt the function that properly belongs to the legislature?

The options available in confronting change demands also have a vital impact on the character of the prescriptive function. Legislation, for example, can be permissive, prohibitory, or regulatory. It can carry affirmative or negative sanctions or can merely be an expression of policy. Through the use of licensing, taxing, and report requirements, the legislature may not only make an immediate determination on a policy issue but can seek to provide for subsequent implementation. Special agencies can be created to maintain continuing surveillance (e.g., fair employment practices commissions). A statute may provide for the government itself to perform a desired task or it may seek to induce others to perform it by persuasion or by offer of reward or assistance (e.g., public housing v. FHA mortgage guarantees). Policy can be formulated in such a manner as to accommodate contending parties— negotiation and compromise are hallmarks of the legislative process. When the legal system deals with complex social or economic change presenting a wide range of legal issues, legislative rather than judical resources assume a vital importance.

CONCLUSION ON LEGISLATIVE-JUDICIAL COMPARISONS IN REGARD TO INITIAL LEGAL RESPONSE

As between the legislative and judicial actors, then, legal response to change conditions is more likely to originate from the judicial forum. The major reason for this appears to be the general unwillingness of the legislature to act in a new area—a wait-and-see attitude born of political and institutional reservations. On the other hand, a variety of weaknesses are noticeable in the judiciary's ability to cope with complex social problems. But this analysis is only suggestive of what might be done for each of the legal subsystems as initial forums for action.

Availability to interests seeking change, capacity to process data so as to permit a creative legal response, and the variables influencing prescriptive behavior all must be empirically delineated.

REACTIVE LEGAL ACTION

As suggested above, the decision by a legal actor in response to a change demand is only the initial stage in an interactive process. Even if an initial response tends to lack the comprehensiveness and expertise desired, it arguably can serve as an impetus to further policy formation. Perhaps it is the limitation of institutional actors that account for the interactive behavior since none of the actors is really equipped to handle the task on its own.

LEGISLATIVE ACTION FOLLOWING INITIAL
JUDICIAL POLICY-MAKING

It may be suggested that initial judicial policy formation tends to produce either of the following consequences: (a) the creation of a legislative acquiescence or apathy, resulting in legislative inaction; or (b) acceleration of the change process by producing greater awareness of the problem, thereby stimulating interest aggregation and articulation, thus generally adding impetus for legislative action. Legislative response may seek to implement, modify, extend, or reverse the judicially fashioned policy; or it may (although not likely at this early stage) be directed against the court itself. The form and extent of legislative response will tend to reflect the same motivational factors suggested earlier, although the changed situation may alter their salience. The initial choice to be faced by the legislature, however, is whether to act at all.

In many cases, judicial decision appears to be an element which can restructure the situation and perhaps affect the legislative orientation. In fact, the judiciary may try to directly or indirectly influence legislative behavior by communicating the need for action (Murphy, 1964). The impact of the judicially fashioned policy on society might itself become an impetus for legislative intervention. It is essential that increased attention be given to the influence of the process itself on policy formation, to the ability of legal actors to influence each other formally or informally and to communicate their needs, to relevant information, and to policy preferences to the other actors in the legal system.

JUDICIAL POLICY-MAKING FOLLOWING LEGISLATIVE ACTION

It is unlikely that either initial legislative activity or reactive legislative action as described above would terminate the process of legal change. Even if the legislature were intermittently to review its actions in light of changed social conditions, disappointed parties in society would probably seek judicial interpretation of the legislative enactment or a determination regarding its constitutionality. And the manner in which the courts exercise their prerogative in the areas of statutory interpretation, constitutional determination, and procedural abstention, will have a vital effect on the character of the legal response to social change situations, influencing not only the role of the judiciary in the process but also that of the legislature.

A literalist approach to the interpretative function, a limited perspective on the role of the courts in constitutional decision-making, or an active use of abstention techniques will act to place a greater burden on the legislature. Alternatively, emphasis on the purpose of a statute, greater acceptance of the political role of the court in constitutional decision-making, and an emphasis on the need for greater access expand the role of the courts as coordinate branches in the policy-making process. It arguably would permit the courts to apply their special attributes and capacities to the task of creative social engineering while serving to stimulate responsive behavior from other legal actors.

Again, inquiry into the motivations for choosing among these alternatives at this stage of the process is essential. But it should also be noted again that, although the same factors discussed above may be operative, their direction and effect might be altered; legislative action has intervened.

An activist model of judicial behavior at this stage of the process again suggests the vital importance of intelligence-gathering for effective policy formation. The judicial actor would require extensive data on the social consequences of legislatively fashioned policy, the possible social impact of suggested policy revisions and the possible reactions of other legal actors which might produce a response directed at the court itself. It is questionable, however, whether the courts presently have the capabilities to process such data adequately even if it were available.

LEGISLATIVE POLICY-MAKING FOLLOWING JUDICIAL REACTION

Even judicial reaction to a legislatively fashioned policy does not necessarily mark an end to the policy-making process. In fact, legislative response to such judicial reaction may be fundamentally different from the legislative reaction to a case of initial judicial policy-making.

The tendency to view the Supreme Court as a court of last resort, the final arbiter from which there is no recourse, ignores the fact that the Court, like all legal institutions, respresents only another stage in the adjustment of legal disputes. Whether making constitutional or interpretative decisions, it can expect to have its determinations reviewed internally by the lower courts, by the administration in the extent to which the decision is implemented, by the public in the character of their compliance, or by Congress in the form of a reaction through constitutional amendment or legislation directed against a particular decision or against the Court itself.

On the other hand, the tendency of studies done thus far to limit their inquiry to negative legislative response has tended to ignore the fact that court action may serve as an impetus to positive legislative action designed to implement the judicial policy decision. Consideration must also be given to the possibility of legislative nonaction as a viable alternative, especially where the judicial actor has accepted the legislative policy in the court's reactive behavior or where the legislature acquiesces to a judicially fashioned policy. On the other hand, nonaction may be the consequence of negative motivational factors. In any case, there is a real need to inquire into the factors that influence the particular form of legislative response and into the actual communication patterns both within the court and the legislature and between these legal institutions at this late state of the legal change process (Murphy, 1962; Stumpf, 1965).

THE DYNAMICS OF CHANGE

While the analysis presented thus far sought to delineate the sequence of activities that constitutes the process of a legal adjustment to social change, it is vital to stress the dynamic character of the process (Sorokin, 1967: 64). Thus we must come to accept the lack of static certainty and the continual process of challenge and response as social change poses new problems for legal adjustment. This does not mean, however, that there is a constantly increasing, uncontrolled stress on the system. The very function of law as a social institution demands that change be managed. Law must be approached as a purposive, goal-orientated system; it must be understood that the behavior of the legal actors is designed to achieve settlement in social disputes—to achieve effective social engineering. Hence, the interactive process seeks to bring about a new stability and a heightened sense of order.

Any legal settlement, however, also alters the social situation, thereby generating new problems. The settlement of a legal dispute is merely a temporary refuge as new interests are aggregated, and new demands are articulated. Acceptance of the dynamics of the legal process as they have been presented in this analysis, and of the rapidity of modern social change, demands a legal system that does not slowly adjust to social problems only after a lag develops. Rather, the system must increasingly anticipate, implement, and direct the change in order to maximize the realization of desired values.

CONCLUSIONS

The legal system, then, has been approached as a dynamic process of recommending, intelligence, and prescribing by each legal actor and the interaction among themselves and with social forces in fashioning legal policy. It must be stressed, however, that it is only a beginning. The framework does not purport to be a comprehensive map of all inter-actions occurring in the legal system. Even as a description of the interactive behavior of the legislative and judicial actors, it requires development and refinement. Nevertheless, it does appear to provide a viable instrument for identifying, organizing, and analyzing the essential considerations involved in legal response to social change. Only by further application, development, and expansion of the framework will its actual worth as a conceptual tool be known.

NOTES

1. The decisional scheme in this analysis is essentially that of Lasswell (1963) and Snyder (1958).

2. Cherryholmes and Shapiro (1969), Jewell and Patterson (1966), and Wahlke and Eulau (1959) provide excellent compilations of the legislative behavior studies.

3. There are numerous compilations of behavioral studies dealing with the motivations behind judicial policy-making. See, e.g., Becker (1964); Grossman and Tanenhaus (1969); Schubert (1965); Symposium (1966); and Wells and Grossman (1966).

REFERENCES

AUERBACH, C. A. et al. (1961) The Legal Process. San Francisco: Chandler.

––– (1959) "Law and social change in the United States." Univ. of California at Los Angeles Law Rev. 6 (July): 520-532.

BECKER, T. L. (1964) Political Behavioralism and Modern Jurisprudence. Chicago: Rand-McNalley.

CHERRYHOLMES, C. and M. SHAPIRO (1969) Representatives and Roll Calls. Indianapolis: Bobbs-Merrill.

CHURCHMAN, C. W. (1961) Prediction and Optimal Decision. Englewood Cliffs, N.J.: Prentice-Hall.

DROR, Y. (1968) Public Policymaking Reexamined. San Francisco: Chandler.

FRIENDLY, H. (1963) 'The gap in law making–judges who can't and legislators who won't." Columbia Law Rev. 63 (May): 787-807.

GROSSMAN, J. and J. TANENHAUS (1969) Frontiers of Judicial Research. New York: John Wiley.

HART, H. M. and A. M. SACKS (1958) The Legal Process: Basic Problems in the Making and Application of Law. Cambridge: Harvard Univ. Press.

JACOB, H. (1965) Justice in America. Boston: Little, Brown.

JEWELL, M. and S. PATTERSON (1966) The Legislative Process in the United States. New York: Random House.

LASSWELL, H. (1963) "The decision process: seven categories of functional analysis," pp. 93-105 in N. W. Polsby, R. A. Dentler, and P. A. Smith (eds.) Politics and Social Life. Boston: Houghton-Mifflin.

LINDBLOM, C. E. (1963) "The science of 'muddling through'," pp. 339-348 in N. W. Polsby, R. A. Dentler, and P. A. Smith (eds.) Politics and Social Life. Boston: Houghton-Mifflin.

LLEWELLYN, K. N. (1930) The Bramble Bush. New York: Columbia Univ. Press.

MURPHY, W. (1964) The Elements of Judicial Strategy. Chicago: Univ of Chicago Press.

––– (1962) Congress and the Court. Chicago: Univ. of Chicago Press.

SCHUBERT, G. (1965) Judicial Policy-Making. Chicago: Scott, Foresman.

SELZNICK, P. (1963) "Legal institutions and social controls." Vanderbilt Law Rev. 17 (December): 79-90.

SIMON, H. (1958) Models of Man. New York: John Wiley.

SYNDER, R.C. (1958) "A decision-making approach to the study of political phenomena," pp. 3-38 in R. Young (ed.) Approaches to the Study of Politics. Evanston: Northwestern Univ. Press.

SOROKIN, P. (1967) "Reasons for sociocultural change and variable recurrent processes," pp. 68-80 in W.E. Moore and R. M. Cook (eds.) Readings in Social Change. Englewood Cliffs, N.J.: Prentice-Hall.

STUMPF, H. (1965) "Congressional response to Supreme Court rulings." J. of Public Law 14: 377-395.

Symposium (1966) "Social science approaches to the judicial process." Harvard Law Rev. 79 (June): 1551-1628.

WAHLKE, J.C. and H. EULAU (1959) Legislative Behavior–A Reader in Theory and Research. Glencoe, Ill.: Free Press.

WELLS, R. and J. GROSSMAN (1966) "The concept of judicial policy making–a critique." J. of Public Law 15: 286-310.

Social Change and Criminal Law

C. RAY JEFFERY
New York University

HISTORICAL DEVELOPMENTS

The impact of social change on law will be discussed in at least two different ways: (1) The impact of urbanization on criminal law and the extension of law into the area of morality. As a result there exists in a heterogeneous society many behaviors which are labelled "criminal" which are contrary to the value systems of a significant part of the population. (2) The impact of the social sciences on law, with the result that psychiatric and sociological concepts designed to rehabilitate the offender have changed the form and the administration of the law.

THE IMPACT OF SOCIAL CHANGE ON LAW AS SOCIAL CONTROL

Criminal law represents the formal means by which control and order are maintained in today's society. Based on a system of formal sanctions, primarily punitive, criminal law assumes many of the functions that in an earlier society were performed informally by the family, church, school, and neighborhood. The courtroom today handles, in some instances, what in a more rural society was handled in the woodshed.

The direction of social change has been variously characterized by social philosophers as folk to urban, mechanical to organic, Gemeinschaft to Gesselschaft, primary to secondary, or sacred to secular (Becker and Boskoff, 1967: 18-32; Jeffery, 1956b, 1959).

The weakness of criminal law as a means of social control is a reflection of the deterioration of the informal controls and the inability of the criminal law to operate effectively in a complex urban setting. As a result of social change, we are involved in a legal system where the rules of conduct are unenforced and unenforceable, and where the law has been overextended into many areas of conduct not before subject to criminal sanction. Writers speak about "crimes without victims" (Schur,

1965) and the "the overcriminalization of the system" (Kadish, 1967) when referring to the extension of criminal sanctions to alcoholism, drug addiction, abortion, and homosexuality. Not only do we use the criminal law to control personal morality, but to control student unrest and racial protests, thus adding to an already overburdened system.

The process by which behavior is labeled deviant or criminal has come to be of concern to criminologists and sociologists in recent years (Becker, 1963; Jeffery, 1956a, 1959; Quinney, 1969), and more attention needs to be paid to the use of criminal law to enforce morality and social welfare (Allen, 1958). The criminal law developed out of a religious-rural tradition, and the purpose of criminal law within an industrial-urban complex must be reappraised.

FROM PUNISHMENT TO DETERRENCE TO REHABILITATION

As a result of the growth of social science during the twentieth century, the criminal law has shifted from social control via punishment and deterrence to social control via rehabilitation and the study of the traits of individual criminals.

Capital punishment came into widespread use from the twelfth century on as a result of the decline of the blood feud. The harsh and arbitrary use of capital punishment during the Middle Ages led to the use of transportation and imprisonment as alternatives to execution, and the classical school of criminology, as exemplified by the writings of Bentham and Beccaria, advocated deterrence as a main rationale of law based on the theme that the punishment should fit the crime, with strict legal definitions of crime and punishment to safeguard the rights of the accused (Radzinowicz, 1966; Mannheim, 1960; Hall, 1945).

The deterrence theory was challenged in the nineteenth century by the positive school, Lombroso, Garofalo, and Ferri, which, reflecting the new science of behavior movement, advocated rehabilitating criminals by means of individualized treatment while rejecting legal definitions of crime and punishment (Randzinowicz, 1966; Mannheim, 1960; Hall, 1945). The positive school has so dominated American criminology that the study of individual offenders and their rehabilitation has come to be the major concern (Hall, 1945; Jeffery, 1956a; Vold, 1958: 39). As a result of the "rehabilitative ideal," we have sick people in place of criminals and hospitals in place of prisons (Allen, 1959; Wootton, 1959: 336; Szasz, 1965). Mechanisms for carrying out the rehabilitative ideal include probation, parole, juvenile courts, sexual psychopath laws, and community-based programs.

Positive criminology makes the following assumptions which form the theoretical structure for our thinking about criminal behavior:

(1) The causes of crime can be found through the study of individual offenders.

(2) Individual offenders can be rehabilitated through the use of psychiatric and sociological concepts.

(3) Punishment is not a successful means to change human behavior.

(4) Criminal behavior can be controlled indirectly through the manipulation of noncriminal behavior, e.g., therapy, job training, and remedial education.

(5) Criminals can be changed by giving them services, rather than through basic research into the behavioral foundations of criminality.

THE FAILURE OF PAST APPROACHES EMPHASIZING THE INDIVIDUAL

THE INDIVIDUAL REHABILITATIVE APPROACH

The success of programs to rehabilitate criminals has been negligible. The recidivism rate of men released from prison has been placed at sixty-seventy percent (Sutherland and Cressey, 1966: 665), and though this figure has been challenged by Glaser (1964: 13-35) as being too high, his own study of the federal penal system documented the failure of therapeutic, educational, and job training programs within the prison system. Glaser concluded that postrelease experiences related to family, employment, and friendships are more crucial in the rehabilitation of criminals than are prisons, the same conclusion Conrad (1965: 64-65) reached from his survey of international correctional practices. A study of the California prison system revealed that the longer a man was in prison, the higher the rate of recidivism (Crowther, 1969: 152). A recent issue of *The Annals* (January, 1969) devoted to "The Future of Corrections" advocated alternatives to imprisonment such as community-based programs, though one writer (Moeller, 1969: 86) found little hard evidence that such programs have been successful in reaching the objectives which they have sought.

Psychotherapy and social casework have failed to reform criminals, as seen in the failure of the Judge Baker Clinic (Witmer and Tufts, 1964: 37-39), the Cambridge-Somerville project (Powers and Witmer, 1951), and the Vocational High School project (Meyer et al., 1966). Several behavioral scientists have written about the lack of evidence to support the claims of a therapeutic approach to behavioral disorders (Berelson and Steiner, 1964: 287; Eysenck, 1961: 712-713; McConnell, 1968). The failure of the therapy-casework model had led some correctional people to turn to group therapy, guided group interaction, and the use of ex-inmates for changing criminals into law-abiding citizens. If criminals learn criminal behavior through contact with criminal attitudes and values, then the way to reform criminals is to use group pressures upholding law-abiding values as a means of changing behavior (Sutherland and Cressey, 1966: 675-680: Joint Commission on Correctional Manpower and Training, 1968). The President's Commission on Law Enforcement and Administration of Justice (1967a: 38-39) found no clear evidence for the success or failure of such programs, and a recent publication by the Joint Commission on Correctional Manpower and Training (1968) was silent on this crucial issue. Since the model is one of treating the individual offender through indirect means, through the manipulation of noncriminal behavior, the prospects for success at a significant level are not great.

A summary of the report on juvenile delinquency by the President's Commission (1967b: 410) concluded that "there are no demonstrable proven methods for reducing the incidence of serious delinquent acts through prevention or rehabilitative procedures." Michael and Adler (1933) concluded that criminology would not be a science until we first developed a science of human behavior. The President's Commission, 37 years later, (1967b: 8) concluded that "until the science of human behavior matures far beyond its present confines, an understanding of delinquency is not likely to be forthcoming." The inability of our criminal justice system to rehabilitate offenders is in no small measure due to our lack of scientific knowledge about human behavior.

The courts in recent years have accepted the "rehabilitative ideal." In Durham v. United States (214 F. 2d 862, 1954), Driver v. Hinnant (356 F. 2d 761, 1966), California v. Robinson (370 U.S. 660, 1962), and Easter v. District of Columbia (361 F. 2d 50, 1966), courts have broadened the scope of mental illness and criminal responsibility and have held that alcoholism and drug addiction are mental illnesses to be treated as illness, rather than crimes to be punished. On the other hand, the failure of rehabilitation has resulted in the court stating in Kent v. United States (383 U.S. 556, 1966) that "there may be grounds for concern that the child receives the worst of both worlds: that he get neither the protections accorded to adults nor the solicitous care and regenerative treatment postulated for children." In re Gault (87 S.Ct. 1428, 1966) Justice Fortas wrote that "the high crime rate among juveniles could not lead to the conclusion that . . . the juvenile system is effective to reduce or rehabilitate offenders." In Powell v. Texas (392 U.S. 514, 1968), the Supreme Court rejected the notion that alcoholics are without responsibility, or that placing a sign saying "hospital" where "jail" stood before is to the benefit of either the alcoholic or the public. In Rouse v. Cameron (373 F. 2d 451, 1967) the court held that persons committed to mental hospitals by reasons of insanity under the Durham rule had a right to treatment, and if treatment is not forthcoming the patient must be released from custody.

We thus arrived at a point in legal history where the offender cannot be placed in prison because the law states he should be rehabilitated, and he cannot be retained in a mental hospital because such institutions fail to rehabilitate.

THE PUNITIVE-DETERRENCE APPROACH

The classical school viewed the criminal law as a means of deterring criminal behavior via punishment. Deterrence has failed, and many criminologists regard punishment as barbaric (Ball, 1955). The rejection of punishment as a means of controlling human behavior has been so complete as to lead to statements such as made in a recent book by Karl Menninger (1968) that punishment is our (the punisher's) need for crime, and our need to displace guilt feelings by punishing criminals.

The statements made in criminology about punishment are contradicted by experimental evidence from behavioral psychology. Experiments in the effect of punishment on behavior have shown that punishment is a powerful means to control behavior (Honig, 1966: 380-477). Punishment, to be effective, must be certain and immediate. However, because of the uncertainty of punishment within the criminal justice system, and because of the long delay between the criminal act and the punishment, the criminal law makes the use of punishment ineffective at best. Very few criminal offenses are cleared by arrest, and, of those arrested, even fewer are sentenced or imprisoned. The President's Commission (1967c: 61) published the following figures:

2,780,000	reported crimes
727,000	arrests
177,000	complaints
160,000	sentences
63,000	imprisoned

The police system is geared to order, law enforcement, and services, and less than twenty percent of police activity involves what can be called serious felonies (Packer, 1966; Wilson, 1968a, 1968b). Congestion, plea bargaining, and administrative inefficiencies have made punishment anything but certain and swift as practiced by our courts (Newman, 1966; President's Commission, 1967d). The police and courts operate on the "apprehend, convict, and rehabilitate the individual after the crime" model, which has failed up till now. Current recommendations, such as hire more policemen, give the police better training, hire more judges and prosecutors, and make use of preventive detention will not change the basic structure of the criminal justice system.

The role of deterrence in criminal law has received little attention in the past fifty years, though Norval Morris (1969: 137-146) and his associates at the University of Chicago Law School have undertaken a project on deterrence and criminal law. To be effective, punishment must be certain, not necessarily severe. The deterrent power of criminal law as an instrument for social control depends on certainty of punishment, which at this stage of development is lacking in both our police and our courts. If correctional agencies have failed to rehabilitate, it is not less true that the police and courts have failed to deter criminal activities.

If we cannot deter criminal behavior via police, courts, and prisons; and if we cannot rehabilitate criminals via correctional programs, what then is the proper relationship between criminal law, behavioral science, and law enforcement?

MODERN APPROACHES THROUGH SOCIAL MANIPULATION

REHABILITATION THROUGH COMMUNITY ACTION PROGRAMS

The thesis that poverty causes crime has been a popular one in criminology. Vold (1958: 169-172) summarized the studies made of poverty and crime by noting that

> from the earlier studies to the present, the conclusion has usually been taken for granted that poverty and unemployment are major factors producing criminality. . . . It would be more logical to conclude that neither poverty nor wealth . . . is a major determining influence in crime and delinquency.

In recent years, poverty and criminality have been reemphasized by the Cloward-Ohlin thesis of differential opportunity structure. The federal government, through the office of Juvenile Delinquency, used the opportunity theory as the basis of its delinquency prevention program (Marris and Rein, 1967). Mobilization for Youth in New York City was based on this theory of delinquent behavior. "A year after the project had entered its action phase, reducing poverty was given first priority in order to prevent and control delinquency" (Brager and Purcell, 1967: 88-89).

Commenting on this theory, the British criminologist Radzinowicz (1966: 98) writes:

> When Cloward and Ohlin speak of criminal opportunities they are thinking primarily of the chance to learn criminal attitudes and techniques. It seems to me, however, that in trying to account for crime in an affluent society we cannot ignore criminal opportunities in another sense—the sheer frequency with which situations present themselves which make crime both tempting and easy.

Speaking of the heavy investment the Ford Foundation made in action programs, Radzinowicz (1965: 30-31) stated that "these schemes are primarily concerned with social policy, social welfare, and social services, and it is essential to emphasize that . . . they should not be identified too closely in the public mind with programs of crime prevention." Marshall Clinard (1968: 157-161) also rejects the idea that poverty causes crime, and he questions the validity of the Cloward-Ohlin thesis.

A total community action program undertaken in Boston, involving the community, family, and gangs, had a negligible impact on delinquency. Miller (1962) points out that the model that was a failure in Boston was used for the total community action approach to delinquency undertaken in the United States in the 1960s.

From a comprehensive study of community action projects, Marris and Rein (1967: 89, 132, 195) concluded that "while projects could claim many individual successess, and may well have increased somewhat the range of opportunities, they did so at great cost and without benefit to perhaps two-thirds of those who sought their help." They found that the poverty program was never primarily concerned with delinquency, since the assumption was made that if poverty were reduced, then ipso facto crime and delinquency would be reduced.

Daniel P. Moynihan (1968: 46, 102, 188), presently the Assistant to the President for Urban Affairs, has published a most critical statement of the poverty program, especially the Mobilization for Youth project and the role of social scientists in the poverty program. He argues that social scientists did not have the knowledge to alleviate poverty and delinquency, and they then became advocates of social reform rather than scientific evaluators of results.

The President's Commission (1967b: 41-56) placed great emphasis on job training and remedial education, yet such an approach to crime prevention is based on indirect controls over behavior via education and employment. The assumption is made that education and employment (one class of behaviors) control delinquency and crime (another class of behaviors). There is no psychological reason why the environmental contingencies controlling educational or employment behavior should control delinquent behavior, and the failure of the poverty program can in part be related to the faulty behavioral analysis involved in its formulation.

CRIME CONTROL AND DIRECT ENVIRONMENTAL ENGINEERING

An adequate model of crime control must:

(a) prevent crime before it occurs, not deal with it after it has occurred;

(b) establish direct controls rather than indirect controls over criminal behavior; and

(c) change the criminal environment in which crimes occur, rather than dealing with the personality of the individual criminal.

The most recent developments in behavioral science have given rise to such concepts as behaviorism, environmentalism, adaptive behavior, systems analysis, and decision theory. Behaviorism has had its origins in the learning theorists in psychology (Kretch, et al., 1969: 287-484), and now has advocates in sociology, public administration, and political science (Handy and Kurtz, 1964; Charlesworth, 1967). Though a lack of space forbids any detailed discussion of behaviorism, its basic ingredients include, among others, a scientific and experimental analysis of behavior, and a view of behavior as a response or adaptation to given environmental conditions. The organism is viewed as an input-output system, with environmental experiences (stimuli) serving as the input, while the nervous-muscular system serves as the output or response system. The individual responds to and operates upon his environment—thus the phrase "operant behavior." The major focus of behaviorism is the adaptation of the organism to the environment through behavior based upon a system of rewards and punishment.

Systems analysis is likewise interested in organism-environment interaction, the interaction of parts to systems, or one system to another system. Decision theory is concerned with the response of an individual so as to maximize gain and minimize loss.

The crucial role of behavior, environment, reward, and punishment in contemporary behavioral science has vast implications for criminal law and law enforcement. The major lesson relevant to criminal law and corrections is that to change the behavior of the individual criminal, we must change the environment to which he responds. The failure of psychotherapy, group counseling, probation, parole, prisons, job training programs, and remedial education programs is in no small measure due to the fact that such programs operate on the individual offender and do not change the environment in which crimes occur.

Jane Jacobs (1961) has pointed out how unsafe our city streets, parks, and buildings are because of the way we make use of urban planning and design. Alexander (1967: 60-109) notes that urban environments have created isolation, alienation, and social deviance, and he advocates a program of urban design which will create human contact at a primary intimate level. Boggs (1965) has demonstrated how crime rates can be studied as properties of environmental opportunities to commit crimes.

If we view criminal behavior as a response to an environmental opportunity to commit a crime, rather than as a psychological or sociological trait of an individual offender, then law enforcement becomes a matter of environmental engineering. If we use a decision-theory model, criminal behavior becomes a matter of potential gain (reward) versus potential loss (punishment), and as our judicial system now operates, the gain outweighs the loss. By making the commission of a criminal act impossible or at least difficult, we would reduce the potential gain to a minimum while increasing the potential loss. This will require extensive use of science and technology in the prevention of crimes, as well as the use of urban design and planning as an integral part of law enforcement and crime control. Police departments would change from agencies "responding to crime after it has occurred" to agencies "preventing crime before it occurs."

The focus of criminal justice administration would change from deterrence and rehabilitation of individual offenders to prevention and control through environmental engineering. The old concepts and practices of furnishing services to inmates, such as are involved in therapy, probation, imprisonment, and community action programs would be replaced with science, technology, urban planning and design, decision theory, and systems analysis.

Criminal law would thus become a part of behaviorism, environmentalism, urban planning, and so forth. It would return to its basic function of deterrence, though in a different form from that in classic criminology. Law would be viewed as a social instrumentality for spelling out the consequences of behavior and for guaranteeing both the consequences and due process in the application of the law. Criminal law would remove itself from the social work-rehabilitative model and assume its historic role as a source of social control, with its emphasis on the external environment, not on the individual offender. Crime as a characteristic of the environment would be researched in place of the rehabilitative emphasis on the individual criminal. The positive school denied the relevance of criminal law either as a means of social control or as a means of guaranteeing due process, and in 1970 we are witnessing the consequences of such a strong commitment to positivistic individualistic criminology.

REFERENCES

ALLEN, F. A. (1959) "Criminal justice, legal values and the rehabilitative ideal." J. of Criminal Law, Criminology, and Police Sci. 50 (September-October): 226-232.
——— (1958) "The borderland of the criminal law: problems of socializing criminal justice." Social Service Rev. 32 (June): 107-119.
ALEXANDER, C. (1967) "The city as a mechanism for sustaining human contact," pp. 60-109 in W. Ewald (ed.) Environment for Man. Bloomington: Indiana Univ. Press.
BALL, J. (1955) "The deterrence concept in criminology and law." J. of Criminal Law, Criminology, and Police Sci. 44 (September-October): 347-352.
BECKER, H. P. and A. BOSKOFF (1957) Modern Sociological Theory. New York: Dryden.
BECKER, H. S. (1963) Outsiders. New York: Free Press.
BERELSON, B. and G. A. STEINER (1964) Human Behavior. New York: Harcourt, Brace & World.
BOGGS, S. (1965) "Urban crime patterns." Amer. Soc. Rev. 30 (December): 899-908.
BRAGER, C. and F. P. PURCELL (1967) Community Action Against Poverty. New Haven: College & Univ. Press.
CHARLESWORTH, J. [ed.] (1967) Contemporary Political Analysis. New York: Free Press.
CLINARD, M. (1968) Sociology of Deviant Behavior. New York: Holt, Rinehart & Winston.

CONRAD, J. (1965) Crime and its Correction. Berkeley: Univ. of California Press.

CROWTHER, C. (1969) "Crimes, penalties, and legislatures." Annals 381 (January): 147-158.

EYSENCK, H. J. (1961) Handbook of Abnormal Psychology. New York: Basic Books.

GLASER, D. (1964) The Effectiveness of a Prison and Parole System. Indianapolis: Bobbs-Merrill.

HALL, J. (1945) "Criminology," pp.342-365 in G. Gurvitch and W. Moore (eds.) Twentieth Century Sociology. New York: Philosophical Press.

HANDY, R. and P. KURTZ (1964) A Current Appraisal of the Behavioral Sciences. Great Barrington: Behavioral Research Council.

HONIG, W. (1966) Operant Behavior. New York: Appleton-Century-Crofts.

JACOBS, J. (1961) The Death and Life of Great American Cities. New York: Random House.

JEFFERY, C. R. (1959) "An integrated theory of crime and criminal behavior." J. of Criminal Law, Criminology, and Police Sci. 49 (March-April): 533-552.

——— (1956a) "The structure of American criminological thinking." J. of Criminal Law, Criminology, and Police Sci. 46 (January-February): 658-672.

——— (1956b) "Crime, law, and social structure." J. of Criminal Law, Criminology, and Police Sci. 47 (November-December): 423-435.

Joint Commission on Correctional Manpower and Training (1968) Offenders as a Correctional Manpower Resource. Washington, D.C.: Government Printing Office.

KADISH, S. H. (1967) "The crisis of overcriminalization." Annals 374 (November): 157-170.

KRETCH, D. et al. (1969) Elements of Psychology. New York: Alfred A. Knopf.

MANNHEIM, H. (1960) Pioneers in Criminology. London: Stevens.

MARRIS, P. and M. REIN (1967) Dilemmas of Social Reform. New York: Atherton.

McCONNELL, J.V. (1968) "Psychoanalysis must go." Esquire (October): 176.

MENNINGER, K. (1968) The Crime of Punishment. New York: Viking.

MEYER, H. J. et al. (1966) Girls at Vocational High. New York: Russell Sage.

MICHAEL, J. and M.J. ADLER (1933) Crime, Law, and Social Science. New York: Harcourt, Brace.

MILLER, W. (1962) "The impact of a total community delinquency control project." Social Problems 10 (Fall): 168-190.

MOELLER, H. G. (1969) "The continuum of correction." Annals 381 (January): 86.

MORRIS, N. and F. ZIMRING (1969) "Deterrence and correction." Annals 381 (January): 137-146.

MOYNIHAN, D. P. (1968) Maximum Feasible Misunderstanding. New York: Free Press.

NEWMAN, D. R. (1966) Conviction. Boston: Little, Brown.

PACKER, H. L. (1966) "The courts, the police, and the rest of us." J. of Criminal Law, Criminology, and Police Sci. 57 (September): 238-243.

POWERS, E. and H. L. WITMER (1951) An Experiment in the Prevention of Delinquency. New York: Columbia Univ. Press.

President's Commission on Law Enforcement and Administration of Justice (1967a) Corrections. Washington, D.C.: Government Printing Office.

――― (1967b) Juvenile Delinquency and Youth Crime. Washington, D.C.: Government Printing Office.

――― (1967c) Science and Technology. Washington, D.C.: Government Printing Office.

――― (1967d) The Courts. Washington, D.C.: Government Printing Office.

QUINNEY, R. (1969) Crime and Justice in Society. Boston: Little, Brown.

RADZINOWICZ, L. (1966) Ideology and Crime. New York: Columbia Univ. Press.

―――(1965) The Need for Criminology. London: Heinemann.

SCHUR, E. H. (1965) Crimes Without Victims. Englewood Cliffs, N.J.: Prentice-Hall.

SUTHERLAND, E. H. and D. R. CRESSEY (1966) Principles of Criminology. Philadelphia: Lippincott.

SZASZ, T. (1965) Psychiatric Justice. New York: Macmillan.

VOLD, G. (1958) Theoretical Criminology. New York: Oxford Univ. Press.

WILSON, J. Q. (1968a) Varieties of Police Behavior. Cambridge: Harvard Univ. Press.

――― (1968b) "Dilemmas of police administration." Public Administration Rev. (September-October): 407-416.

WITMER, H. L. and E. TUFTS (1964) The Effectiveness of Delinquency Prevention Programs. Washington, D.C.: Children's Bureau.

WOOTTON B. (1959) Social Science and Social Policy. New York: Macmillan.

The Supreme Court and Social Change

A Preliminary Inquiry

JOEL B. GROSSMAN
University of Wisconsin

LACK OF RELEVANT LITERATURE

Although it is frequently the subject of scholarly and political discussions, there is surprisingly little empirical evidence available to support assertions made about the Supreme Court's ability to influence social change. With some exceptions, the Supreme Court does not openly discuss this question in its written opinions. However, it is difficult to imagine that the justices are not concerned with the impact of their decisions. More likely they feel restrained by the limits of their role to discussing only the legal rights of the parties to each case. But it cannot be far from their minds and occasionally their concerns reach the surface.

One reason why the Court's effectiveness as an agent of social change is not much discussed by the justices is that they operate under a set of assumptions which renders such discussion unnecessary. For official purposes at least, the justices tend to assume that once the nation's highest court has made a decision there will be ready and willing compliance from those to whom the decision is directed. But this overlooks the probability that most social changes occur as the incremental result of multi-institutional and societal forces rather than as a direct result of a particular Supreme Court decision or set of decisions. It also overlooks the built-in opportunities for noncompliance and evasion which characterize the American judicial bureaucracy. The Supreme Court rarely has either the first or last word on a subject. It

Author's Note: *The author wishes to express his indebtedness to Kenneth M. Dolbeare for helpful comments on this manuscript.*

usually enters a controversy in peripheral fashion and decides only certain dimensions of that controversy. Its policies may guide, but will rarely determine, the ultimate outcome of events. A decision may provide legal, moral, or symbolic support for a particular cause, and may offer tactical advantages to one side. Victory in the Supreme Court may be of crucial advantage to those seeking to advance or obstruct social change, but it is rarely a good predictor of whether that change will come about.

Analysis of the Court's role as an agent of social change can profitably begin by exploring two related but theoretically distinct levels of behavior: First, when, why, and under what circumstances is the Court likely to make a decision supporting social change? Second, what is the Court's capacity to bring about changes in behavior and attitudes? Figure 1 provides an overall schematic model of these two phases and suggests the points of linkage between them (Grossman, 1969).

VARIABLES CAUSING THE COURT TO FORMULATE POLICY CHANGES

Defining the circumstances in which the Court is likely to formulate a change in policy requires consideration of two sets of variables: the demands on the Court for social change policies, and the responses of the justices, which are best characterized as internal decision-making variables.

DEMANDS ON THE COURT FOR SOCIAL CHANGE POLICIES

The internal rules of the Court, as well as its constitutional limits, discourage it from formulating policies beyond the scope of conflict defined by the litigants. A great part of the responsibility for defining alternative policy choices and problem solutions rests with those who bring or defend cases before the Court, and with those who participate in the litigation as *amicus curiae*. The Court is not totally restrained from considering solutions or policies other than those defined by the litigants, but it normally confines its rulings within these bounds. Given the large number of cases which reach the Court's docket each year, and its virtually complete discretion in choosing which cases to decide, the Court is never forced to hear a particular case or decide a particular issue (Hakman, 1969; Casper, 1969; Barker, 1967).

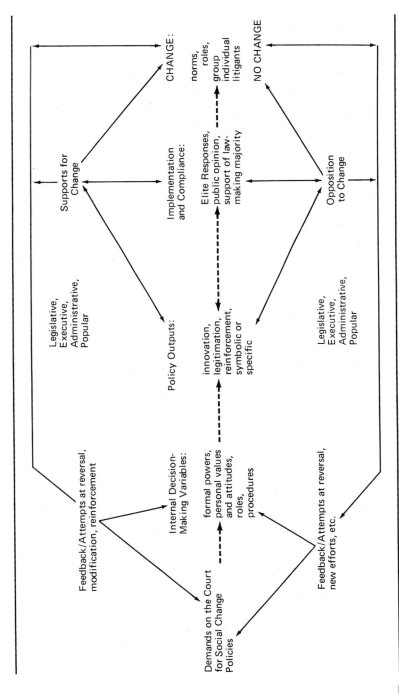

Figure 1: THE SUPREME COURT AND SOCIAL CHANGE: A SCHEMATIC MODEL

Feedback/Attempts at reversal, modification, reinforcement

Supports for Change

Legislative, Executive, Administrative, Popular

CHANGE:

norms, roles, group individual litigants

Internal Decision-Making Variables:

formal powers, personal values and attitudes, roles, procedures

Policy Outputs:

innovation, legitimation, reinforcement, symbolic or specific

Implementation and Compliance:

Elite Responses, public opinion, support of law-making majority

Demands on the Court for Social Change Policies

Feedback/Attempts at reversal, new efforts, etc.

Opposition to Change

Legislative, Executive, Administrative, Popular

NO CHANGE

The Supreme Court has less control of its docket than many other political actors, but this is a difference which is often exaggerated. Politicians are continually responding to demands from constituents or from other politicians, and many, if not most, policies sought by nonlegal political actors are formulated within the context of rules, norms, and pressures which may be every bit as constraining as those felt by judges. Where the real difference may lie is in three respects: first, in the option open to politicians but not generally to judges to *anticipate* and work out solutions for problems in advance of the necessity of doing so; second, in the greater opportunity politicians have—admittedly not always utilized—to obtain maximum information about the need for particular policies and about the problems to be encountered in implementing those policies; and third, in the greater discretion which politicians may have as to the timing of the policy decisions.

Demands for social change which come to the Supreme Court are usually framed as demands for change in legal doctrine. Such demands are likely to be most effective when they are clearly articulated and when the Court is effectively informed of the nature of the problem and the proposed remedy, when the legal doctrines being attacked have been discredited by past decisions or have demonstrated their unworkability, and when the counterdemands—e.g., the responses to those seeking the aid of the Supreme Court—conflict with a prevailing ideological commitment of the Court.

INTERNAL DECISION-MAKING VARIABLES

There are basically four clusters of variables here which *may* have an impact on the Court's decision to respond positively or negatively to demands for social change. The first cluster is best described as the *formal powers of the Court,* including the accumulated traditions of judicial power and common law inherent powers of judges, the specific constitutional and statutory guidelines within which—and by which—a particular case must be decided, and the "state of the law" at the time of the decision.

Not even the Court's strongest supporters at the Constitutional Convention, or in the ratification debates, conceived of it as a primary agent of social change. Many saw its function largely as a deterrent to changes in the prevailing allocation of economic and political resources —the last bastion of private property, if need be. On the other hand, as

McCloskey (1960) has noted, the Court's interest in protecting capitalism meant that it was also supporting the concept of nationalism—in itself a great social change concept of the time.

The great powers of the Court—judicial review of national and state legislation—are essentially negative in their operation and not openly conducive to creative policy formation. However, these powers can be, and have been, used not only in pursuit of positive goals, but even to support innovation. The Court's flexibility in interpreting the words of the Constitution gives it an opportunity to proclaim certain values as superior to others, and to offer important symbolic support for those who wish to advance the values a majority of justices prefer.

Once the Court becomes involved in a particular issue, it often has repeated opportunities to contribute to policy in that area. Not infrequently a Court that began by a negative exercise of power is drawn increasingly into positive policy-making to fill the void which its negative decision has created, or to clarify the ambiguities inherent in continuously negative policy decisions.

The "state of the law" affects the potential policy powers of the Court in a particular case, since the justices' views of what can be done is likely to be at least a partial function of where the law presently stands and where it has been—or should be—going. Likewise, the justices will have a keen appreciation of the legitimacy of their changing a particular law or doctrine. The role of precedents can be overstated, since the Supreme Court is constantly reversing, amending, modifying, distinguishing, or forgetting about precedents which no longer seem adequate. Precedents in some areas of the law are likely to have a greater staying power or legitimacy—and are therefore more difficult to disregard—than in other areas. Likewise, there are certain legal or constitutional doctrines which, through constant reiteration and approval by succeeding generations of judges, seem impervious to change.

The Second Variable

That the personal *values and backgrounds of the individual justices* constitute an important variable is no longer open to question (Grossman and Tanenhaus, 1969; Pritchett, 1968). But defining their particular role and importance in the policy-making process is a more difficult task. To some extent the intrusion of personal values is a function of the aforementioned state of the law. Where the law is clear and relevant to modern conditions, or extremely venerable and difficult to change, an individual justice will have less opportunity to consider his own notions of right and justice. Where the law is unclear, unstable, or clearly unworkable, the personal values of a justice may have the opportunity of greater influence. Whether or not a particular doctrine is considered open to change or to the intrusion of a justice's personal values is probably a function of the justice's perceptions about proper judicial functioning and about the state of the law in a particular field.

There is no necessary connection between the reliance by judges on their personal values and the inevitability of certain policy outcomes—or the inevitability of social change. Current criticisms of the Supreme Court from the political right have alleged that if the justices followed their own values less and the precedents more, they would be making more conservative decisions. Such criticisms are correct, but miss the point that following precedents is not always more conservative, nor following one's own values more liberal. Social change is not inevitably liberal.

The Third Variable

The third decision variable likely to affect social change outputs consists of the *role perceptions of the justices,* particularly those perceptions which concern the proper role of the Court in a democratic society (Grossman and Tanenhaus, 1969: 12-14; Grossman, 1965; Becker, 1964; Grossman, 1962). A current justice who believes it a major responsibility of the Court to see that justice is "done," who believes that the Court has a special responsibility to protect the rights of persons or groups disadvantaged by the political process, and who believes that the Court has a responsibility to democratize the political process, is a justice who is today playing a social change role. Role perceptions are related to, but analytically distinct from, a judge's values and attitudes. Sometimes role perceptions and values are mutually reinforcing, as in the case of Brandeis, a liberal and dedicated supporter of the doctrine of judicial self-restraint, or in the case of Douglas, a political liberal and an opponent of the more confining aspects of the self-restraint role. Sometimes values and role perceptions may be in conflict, as with Holmes, a political conservative whose dedication to self-restraint on the Court made him a liberal in his time, or in the case of Frankfurter, a political liberal whose dedication to self-restraint made him a conservative on the Court (Freund, 1961; Mendelson, 1960; Grossman, 1962).

Role expectations of and by the justices change over time, but most of the socializing into role norms which lawyers and judges undergo tends to be conservative—primarily, though not exclusively—in a procedural sense. Strict adherence and allegiance to many procedural rules, and to the norms of continuity and predictability, would make social change through law virtually impossible. Likewise, strict adherence to the norms of the judicial self-restraint role reduces the options which a judge otherwise interested in promoting social change may employ. Self-restraint by judges and social change are not totally incompatible in situations where the major innovations are coming from legislative bodies, and where the Court's function is merely to ratify or legitimate such actions. During the period from 1890 to 1937, it was the lack of self-restraint on the part of conservative judges which proved to be the most effective obstacle to progressive economic regulation.

The Fourth Variable

The fourth and final set of decision variables affecting the Supreme Court's role in inducing social change consists of *the Court's internal and external operating procedures.* These procedures do not have a uniform effect on the creation or implementation of social change policy; different procedural variables would seem to have had a different impact over time, and on different policy questions (Schmidhauser, 1960; Pt. III).

The way in which the Court conducts its business is probably not conducive to positive social change policy-making. Its size and small professional staff limits its capacity to hear a large number of cases, and also limits the information it can obtain about those cases—both in terms of quantity and quality. For those cases which it does decide, its method and form of communicating its decisions severely reduces its receptive audience. It has a limited ability to receive and act on feedback information. There is an absence of effective powers of implementation, and few credible sanctions for enforcing upopular polices. The Court tends to respond slowly and laboriously to demands and thus lacks the strategic element of timing in its policy pronouncement. Events over which the Court has no control frequently change the realities of a case, but the Court may feel an obligation to decide the case in its original form. The Court cannot always act when needed, although sometimes, as in the present litigation over the constitutionality of capital punishment, events are suspended until the Court decides. Many, if not most, governmental policy decisions come in response to some sort of demand and are limited by the exigencies of time and events. But the court as policy-maker is probably more restricted than most, and its capacities for bringing about change are limited accordingly.

To the extent that the justices of the Supreme Court operate solely as individuals, responding case-by-case to the problems before them, the Court is not likely to exercise a purposeful policy role except by accident. But where policy-oriented justices seek to mobilize their brethren to form majorities on certain issues, they are more likely to be cognizant of the importance of the factors listed above, and more likely manipulate those factors toward policy ends. Murphy, Danelski, and others have suggested a variety of weapons available to the policy-oriented judge, but little is known of the actual recognition or use of these weapons by the justices, except by inference from their opinions or from the occasional insight afforded by the private papers of a deceased justice (Murphy, 1964; Danelski, 1960, 1964).

IDENTIFYING RELEVANT SOCIAL CHANGES

An inquiry into the capacity of the Supreme Court to influence change requires, first, some effort at identifying the sorts of changes that could conceivably take place and be attributed in some way to judicial policies. Although greater specification will ultimately be required, it is best at this point to identify two basic dimensions—changes in behavior, and changes in beliefs and attitudes.

CHANGES IN BEHAVIOR

Behavior changes can be conceptualized in several ways. First, it is necessary to distinguish between mass and elite behavior. One characteristic of most Supreme Court policy decisions is that they are directed, at least in the first instance, toward other judges, public officials, and some elite groups. The precise role of elite groups in transmitting, implementing, and enforcing policy directives which call for change in the behavior of ordinary persons is only vaguely understood. We know more about the conditions under which elites may comply with Supreme Court decisions, and therefore about social changes which require primarily elite rather than mass responses. We have little knowledge of the attitudes toward compliance of ordinary people not in positions of official responsibility.

A second dimension or level of analysis of changes in behavior would include individual behavior changes more or less limited to the persons involved in the litigation and the particular facts in dispute, changes which are characteristic of larger numbers of persons, or groups, and which involve patterns of behavior rather than one-time changes, and, finally, changes of the second type which also involve changes in norms or role expectations of a particular group or segment of society and which are therefore likely to have longer-term effects.

A third type of change would concentrate not so much on the numbers of people involved as on the substantive effects of certain changes—in particular, changes in the structure of political, social, economic or legal institutions, and changes in existing patterns of resource allocation. Structural changes may be ends in themselves, but they are more likely to be instrumental or symbolic, designed to aid in the promotion of a particular type of behavior change or to at least give the appearance of such a change. The Supreme Court may have little or nothing to say about the original wisdom or purpose of a particular institutional structure, but its decisions may have a great impact on the way in which these institutions operate in general, or on certain particular practices. Those institutions which are set up under the Constitution, or which make decisions that raise certain types of issues, are most likely to come under Court scrutiny. The courts and the Bar are likely to come under the closest scrutiny, since policing their internal procedures is both a statutory and inherent power of the Supreme Court. Other institutions are likely to have only certain aspects of their institutional life regulated by the Supreme Court.

Courts can affect the allocation of resources in our society in a variety of way—by changes in the structure of those institutions which do the allocating, by changes in the procedures of allocation, by changing the priority of values to be followed, and by forbidding certain types of allocations. Resource allocation may be an end in itself, or merely instrumental in seeking other goals. Courts do not, of course, have the legislative power of appropriation, but they can by their decisions induce or retard the expenditure of large sums of money. As the history of the pre-New Deal Court shows, the justices can be supremely effective for an extended period of time in preventing a popular majority from allocating its resources in a particular way.

CHANGES IN BELIEFS, ATTITUDES AND SYMBOLS

These changes are closely related to changes in behavior, but analytically distinct. While laws are normally intended to produce behavior rather than belief change, frequently changes in attitudes and beliefs are indispensable catalysts of behavior change. Conversely, attitudes and values are also affected by behavior. Persons who feel compelled by rule, law, or norm to behave in a certain way may eventually come to justify such behavior as a means of removing or ameliorating internal tension— e.g., congnitive dissonance—(Festinger, 1957; Schur, 1968: ch. 3; Muir, 1967).

For most persons not involved in the details of a law suit or politically or legally knowledgeable about the Supreme Court, a judicial policy decision is likely to have a primarily symbolic effect. Political scientists have good evidence of the nonissue orientation of voters who are not involved or specially educated in politics; most citizens make their political judgments on the basis of personalities, vague ideas about the issues separating the candidates for office, traditional and hereditary party affiliations, and a large amount of misinformation (Campbell et al., 1960). The little evidence available indicates that citizens are not any more knowledgeable about the Supreme Court, and we would expect that their understanding of the Court's decisions would thus be primarily in symbolic terms (Dolbeare, 1967; Kessel, 1966; Murphy and Tanenhaus, 1969). This being the case (or at least a tenable hypothesis), we might assume that to the extent the Court can provide effective symbolic representation of certain values, it is likely to have some impact in promoting the behavior which these symbolic values may represent.

Measuring changes in behavior and attitudes presents a more complex problem than identifying the parameters of change in qualitative fashion. Of the two dimensions involved—identifying and measuring changes in behavior and attitudes, and attributing such changes to a particular set of causal variables—the second is undoubtedly more difficult to achieve with the existing tools of social science. Identifying and measuring the extent of particular changes requires some knowledge of the state of behavior at a particular time, the substantive changes made in observable behavior by the principles involved, the degree of acceptance or rejection of the intended changes by these principal actors, the intended or unintended by-products of such changes, and the main feedbacks which these changes produce.

Attributing change to a particular causal variable, or set of variables, may eventually be done most effeciently with quantitative causal modeling techniques now being developed (Cnudde and McCrone, 1966, 1967; Alker, 1966; Bell, 1969). For the present, however, the emphasis must be on the generation of data which can be suitably used by such techniques.

VARIABLES DETERMINING SUPREME COURT INFLUENCE

In what ways can the Supreme Court bring about changes in behavior and belief? The prerequisite action is the issuance of a decision which formulates new legal rules or legitimizes old ones in the context of a particular case. Levine and Becker (1969) have argued that the primary policy power of the Supreme Court comes from its ability to manipulate symbols, and others have suggested that the primary power of any policy-maker is the ability to authoritatively redefine the issues which are to be decided and the rules by which they will be decided. Political power may also be exercised by increasing the scope of conflict; by making a national issue out of a local issue, the Court could bring into play additional forces which may provide help for the party or cause which the Court favors (Schattschneider, 1960).

The Court can perform any of the above-mentioned tasks in a variety of ways, including the refusal to decide certain cases. Among those cases which it decides, the Court can seek to influence change:

(1) by a conscious and explicit program of innovation which may specify particular behavior changes or which may only indicate new symbols or values to be followed;

(2) by reinforcement of prior policy decisions seeking change against challenges to their authority or legitimacy;

(3) by reinforcement or legitimation of the change oriented policies of other governmental agencies or of important groups in society;

(4) by specific invalidation or symbolic challenges to social change processes or policies.

The Court can offer some limited support to social change by not deciding a case where its refusal to decide upholds or reinforces a lower court decision which itself favors change by legitimizing a governmental change policy, and also by refusing to decide a case in which a lower court decision has gone against forces seeking to preserve the status quo.

The Court's decisions may also have a differential effect on social change depending on certain related characteristics, which can be stated in the form of hypotheses (Krislov, 1965; Levine and Becker, 1969; Evan, 1965; Schur, 1968; Miller, 1965; Manwaring, 1963; Reich and Wasby, 1968).

Policy decisions may have a greater impact on change if:

(1) the decision clearly and unambiguously delineates the rights and obligations of *all* persons whose behavior is subject to change as a result of the decision;

(2) the number of alternative options open to persons affected by a policy decision is kept to a minimum except for a necessary face-saving option;

(3) the decision is self-executing, rather than one which requires an increasing number of other persons to get involved in its implementation;

(4) the decision provides reinforcement for a previous innovative policy, including the application of sanctions;

(5) the decision is perceived as authoritative by those at whom it is directed, or by others affected by it;

(6) compliance with the decision is not dependent on the transfer or reallocation of resources by other agencies of government;

(7) the decision is supportable on acceptable ideological grounds and does not conflict with pervasive counterideolgies;

(8) responsibility for compliance with the decision is federal rather than state, centralized rather than decentralized;

(9) the decision engages the self-interested support of the President or Congress, or both;

(10) the decision requires change of a negative kind—e.g., to end a certain practice—rather than change which requires positive or creative thinking;

(11) the decision purports to regulate behavior of a role incumbent whose role is defined primarily by law rather than by custom or tradition;

(12) the decision does not require the direct redistribution of resources by those opposed to the policy.

The Court can, of course, have no influence over social change if it refuses to issue appropriate policy directives, but the mere issuance of those directives is frequently not a sufficient force to bring about such change, except where the policy requires only a change in legal doctrine without accompanying behavioral or attitudinal change, where the policy is directed solely at the workings of the federal judiciary, or where the policy is a post-hoc ratification or legitimation of changes already accomplished. For most other types of changes, the ultimate impact of the Court's policy decision depends on its reception by a number of *elite intermediaries* whose interests may or may not coincide with those of the Court.

How a particular directive is received by those elite groups depends on their receptiveness to the values embodied in the policy directive, the costs to them of trying to secure compliance, their own commitments to change, and a host of other factors. Lower court judges—both state and federal—legislative bodies and officials, school board members and school principals, prison officials, police officials, military commanders, and federal and state administrative-executive officials seem to be the most frequent recipients of Supreme Court policy directives. Discretion in carrying out these directives varies according to law, and in practice. Directives which order officials to refrain from continuing a certain practice allow a minimum of discretion. Directives which state that a particular practice is to be discontinued, but do not specify who is to discontinue it other than in the case of the litigants, allow a larger discretion. Directives that require positive, innovative, or creative actions, and the utilization of new resources, permit a far greater discretion.

A similar role may be played by those groups which tend to represent a particular segment of the population in one or more court cases. If these groups have exhausted the major part of their resources on the litigation itself, they may have little left with which to pursue compliance at the local level, or with which to fight counterattacks on the legitimacy or enforceability of the decision which they had won in court. Not infrequently, the lawyers or groups which represent certain causes have little or no interest in follow-ups at a lower level and the thrust of a policy directive may be lost for want of effective local support. In some cases, such as those dealing with prayers and Bible reading in the schools, the interests of persons which sought a particular policy directive are satisfied to pursue compliance in their own locales and unable or unwilling to expend resources to secure compliance elsewhere. (Levine and Becker, 1969; Dolbeare and Hammond, 1969; Becker, 1969). Finally, for many persons, the satisfactions of a symbolic victory are too important to risk losing by involvement in the pursuit of a compliance which carries with it many frustrations and no assurance of ultimate victory (Levine and Becker, 1969; Casper, 1969).

In the final analysis, control over change comes to those who can mobilize their forces and resources after, as well as before, a Supreme Court decision, to those who can exercise some influence over information about what the Court said and how it said it and to those who are willing to risk losing a symbolic victory in pursuit of a material triumph. Precisely how, when, and where the mobilization of resources would be most advantageous to those who wish to use a Court decision to bring about change is an empirical question for which there is no ready answer. But I suspect that, whatever its shortcomings as a general theory of politics, group theory would provide some good guidelines to the acquisition and interpretation of such data.

Two further environmental variables which have a likely effect on the Supreme Court's impact on social change remain to be mentioned. First, the impact of public opinion, and second, the support for or opposition to the Court's policies exhibited by what Dahl once called the "national lawmaking majority." Most Court decisions do not have any impact on public opinion one way or the other. Less than half of the population has any views about the Court, and barely fifteen percent may have some specific knowledge of Court decisions. Yet those who have some specific knowledge probably include the opinion leaders of the community, and their views of the Court may be effectively transmitted to their constituents. Where negative views about a specific decision, or about the Court as an institution, become pervasive enough in a particular locale, the elites of that community will have greater leeway for ignoring policy directives. By and large, the Court's policies are best implemented in an atmosphere of public disinterest. As Dolbeare (1967) and others have argued, when the public becomes concerned, it usually is in opposition to a particular decision—or to what the Court believes a public decision to have been.

Dahl argued that the Court is most effective when it is giving support to the policies of the national lawmaking majority, less effective but not stymied where Court policies are different from those of a large number of the lawmaking majority but where opposition is dispersed or incapable of effective mobilization, and least effective where an effective majority can be mobilized against the Court (Dahl, 1958). Several distinctions must be made, however, to operationalize this theory. First, the numerical requirement for effective opposition to a Court policy varies with the type of policy pronouncement; invalidation of a congressional statute requires a constitutional amendment for reversal, whereas a statutory decision can be changed by Congress with only a simple majority. Second, vocal and visible opposition to a Court policy by even a small plurality of the lawmaking majority may be sufficient to encourage noncompliance among the constituents of the legislative opponents. Third, even where there is majority opposition to a specific decision, there may be little or no interference with compliance or impact if those to whom the decision has been initially directed have felt obliged to comply as a matter of law, or who have complied quickly because of basic agreement with the policy directive. Effective mobilization to reverse or obstruct a Court policy is much more difficult than mere vocal objection, as the aftermath of the Reapportionment cases and the demise of the Dirksen Amendment have shown (Dixon, 1968; Baker, 1966). On the other hand, mobilization of substantial opposition by the lawmaking majority may effectively support unenthusiastic or minimal compliance with the letter rather than the spirit of a policy decision. The failure of the Court's efforts to place effective restrictions on the broad range of police behavior seems attributable to several factors—the mobilization of local support for the police, the organization and "politization" of the police in response to what they perceive as threats to their integrity, and the fact that the vast majority of police actions do not result in criminal trials and are therefore invisible and immune from Court sanction (Packer, 1969; Yale Law Journal, 1967).

REFERENCES

ALKER, H. R., Jr. (1966) "Causal inferences and political analysis," in J. L. Bernd (ed.) Mathematical Applications in Political Science. Dallas: Southern Methodist Univ. Press.

BAKER, G. (1966) The Reapportionment Revolution. New York: Random House.

BARKER, L. (1967) "Third parties in litigation." J. of Politics 29.

BECKER, T. L. [ed.] (1969) The Impact of Supreme Court Decisions. New York: Oxford Univ. Press.

——— (1964) Political Behaviorism and Modern Jurisprudence. Chicago: Rand-McNally.

BELL, R. (1969) "The determinants of psychological involvement in politics: a causal analysis." Midwest J. of Pol. Sci. 13: 237-253.

CAMPBELL, A., P. CONVERSE, W. MILLER, and D. STOKES (1960) The American Voter. New York: John Wiley.

CASPER, J. (1969) "Lawyers before the supreme court in civil liberties and civil rights cases, 1957-66: recruitment and goals." Delivered at the Annual Meeting of the American Political Science Association.

CNUDDE, C. and D. McCRONE (1967) "Toward a communications theory of democratic political development: a causal model." Amer. Pol. Sci. Rev. 61: 72-79.

——— (1966) "The linkage between constituency attitudes and congressional voting behavior: a causal model." Amer. Pol. Sci. Rev. 60: 68-72.

DAHL, R. A. (1958) "Decision-making in a democracy: the role of the supreme court as a national policy-maker." J. of Public Law 6: 279-295.

DANELSKI, D. J. (1964) A Supreme Court Justice is Appointed. New York: Random House.

——— (1960) "The influence of the chief justice in the decisional process," pp. 497-508 in W. Murphy and H. C. Pritchett (eds.) Courts, Judges, and Politics. New York: Random House.

DIXON, R. G. (1968) Democratic Representation. New York: Oxford Univ. Press.

DOLBEARE, K. M. (1967) "The public views the supreme court," pp. 194-212 in Jacob (ed.) Law, Politics, and the Federal Courts. Boston: Little, Brown.

——— and P. HAMMOND (1969) "Local elites, the impact of judicial decisions, and the process of change." Delivered at Annual Meeting of the American Political Science Association.

EVAN, W. (1965) "Law as an instrument of social change," pp.288-292 in A. W. Gouldner and S. M. Miller (eds.) Applied Sociology. New York: Free Press.

FESTINGER, L. (1957) A Theory of Cognitive Dissonance. Stanford: Stanford Univ. Press.

FREUND, P. (1961) "Mr. Justice Brandeis: portrait of a liberal judge," pp. 116-144 in P. Freund (ed.) The Supreme Court of the United States. Cleveland: Meridian Books.

GROSSMAN, J. B. (1965) Lawyer and Judges: The ABA and the Politics of Judicial Selection. New York: John Wiley.

——— (1962) "Role-playing and the analysis of judicial behavior: the case of Mr. Justice Frankfurter." J. of Public Law 11: 285-309.

——— and J. TANENHAUS (1969) "The renascence of public law," pp. 3-26 in J. B. Grossman and J. Tanenhaus (eds.) Frontiers of Judicial Research. New York: John Wiley.

HAKMAN, N. (1969) "The Supreme Court's political environment: the processing of noncommercial litigation," pp. 199-254 in J. B. Grossman and J. Tanenhaus (eds.) Frontiers of Judicial Research. New York: John Wiley.

KESSEL, J. (1966) "Public perceptions of the supreme court." Midwest J. of Pol. Sci. 10: 167-191.

KRISLOV, S. (1965) The Supreme Court in the Political Process. New York: Macmillan.

LEVINE, J. P. and T. L. BECKER (1969) "Toward and beyond a theory of Supreme Court impact." Presented to the Annual Meeting of the American Political Science Association.

MANWARING, D. (1963) Render Unto Caesar. Chicago: Univ. of Chicago Press.

McCLOSKEY, R. G. (1960) The American Supreme Court. Chicago: Chicago Univ. Press.

MENDELSON, W. (1960) Justices Black and Frankfurter: Conflict in the Court. Chicago: Univ. of Chicago Press.

MILLER, A. S. (1965) "On the need for 'impact analysis' of Supreme Court decisions." Georgetown Law J. 53: 365-401.

MUIR, W. K., Jr. (1967) Prayer in the Public Schools: Law and Attitude Change. Chicago: Univ. of Chicago Press.

MURPHY, W. F. (1964) Elements of Judicial Strategy. Chicago: Univ. of Chicago Press.

——— and J. TANENHAUS (1969) "Public opinion and the United States Supreme Court: a preliminary mapping of some prerequisites for court legitimation of regime changes," pp. 273-303 in J. B. Grossman and J. Tanenhaus (eds.) Frontiers of Judicial Research. New York: John Wiley.

PACKER, H. (1969) The Limits of the Criminal Sanction. Palo Alto: Stanford Univ. Press.

PRITCHETT, C. H. (1968) "Public law and judicial behavior." J. of Politics 30: 480-509.

REICH and WASBY (1968) in D. Everson (ed.) The Supreme Court as Policy-Maker: Three Studies on the Impact of Judicial Decisions. Carbondale, Ill.: Public Affairs Research Bureau of Southern Illinois University.

SCHATTSCHNEIDER, E. E. (1960) The Semi-Sovereign People. New York: Holt, Rinehart & Winston.

SCHMIDHAUSER, J. (1960) The Supreme Court: Its Politics, Personalities, and Procedures. New York: Holt, Rinehart & Winston.

SCHUR, E. (1968) Law and Society: A Sociological View. New York: Random House.

Yale Law Journal (1967) "Interrogations in New Haven: the impact of *Miranda*." 76: 1521-1648.

Law as a Tool of Directed Social Change

A Framework for Policy-Making

YEHEZKEL DROR
The RAND Corporation

The use of law as a tool of directed social change is widespread in all contemporary societies whether underdeveloped or postindustrial, democratic or totalitarian. But both our systematic knowledge on how to use effectively and efficiently law in order to achieve more of our goals and our practical state of the art of doing so approximate zero.

One set of reasons for this state of affairs includes various factors diverting attention from the uses of law as a tool of directed social change. These are, for instance, metaphysical concepts of law, purely formal concepts of law, and preoccupation with other functions of law such as stabilization, prediction-reinforcement, power restraint, and authority control. But the long list of distinguished classic and modern scholars who have devoted their efforts to the study of law and social change and who have made important contributions to many aspects of the subject[1] (other than a comprehensive policy-oriented theory of law as a tool of directed social change) precludes explanation of our theoretic ignorance in terms of lack of high-quality efforts. Similary, the use of law as a tool of directed social change in a large number of jurisdictions precludes explanation of our state-of-the-art weaknesses in terms of lack of experience.

Author's Note: *Any views expressed in this paper are those of the author. They should not be interpreted as reflecting the views of The RAND Corporation or the official opinion or policy of any of its governmental or private research sponsors.*

Rather, it seems that the basic difficulties of studying and improving the use of law as a tool of directed social change result from the fact that law by itself is only one component of a large set of policy instruments and usually cannot and is not used by itself. Therefore, focusing of exclusive attention on law as a tool of directed social change is a case of tunnel vision, which lacks the minimum perspective necessary for making sense from the observed phenomena. Furthermore, the frames-of-appreciation of both policymaking and social science (which today enjoy a near monopoly over the study of law and social change) are inadequate for dealing with the prescriptive and policy-oriented aspects of law as an instrument of social direction.

What is necessary is a redefinition of the subject of "law as a tool of directed social change" in two main directions: (1) as a subcomponent of the study of social policy instruments; and (2) as a subcomponent of normative policy analysis.

LAW AND OTHER SOCIAL POLICY INSTRUMENTS

A first required step on the way to examination of the uses of law as a tool of directed social change within an adequate framework of social policy instruments involves consideration of law within the legal system.

The main components of the legal system can in part be classified for our purposes as follows:

(a) Substantive law: constitutional, statutory, judge-made, administrative.

(b) Procedural law: constitutional, statutory, judge-made, administrative.

(c) Personnel: judges, lawyers, legislators, police, other law enforcing and law administrating persons.

(d) Organizations: legislature, court system, police, legal firms, administrative agencies.

(e) Resources: budgets, information and information processing capacities, physical facilites.

(f) Decision rules and decision habits: formal, informal, implicit.

Even though this classification does not cover all aspects (e.g., distinction by jurisdictions and clienteles), it is sufficient for bringing out both the richness and the complex overlappings and interdependencies in the legal system. My main point here is that each one of the components of the legal system is a potential policy instrument. Indeed, in most circumstances, utilization of any one or few of these components as tools of directed change in isolation from the others will at best be very inefficient, usually useless, and often counterproductive.

Therefore, for better use of law as a tool of directed social change, it is essential in each case to examine carefully the interdependencies between the various components of the relevant legal systems, the interrelations between these components and the target phenomena, and the feasibility and costs (including political feasibility and costs) of changing those components of the legal system which are more salient for the target phenomena. On the basis of such an examination, a preferable set of leverage points in the legal system should be identified, to be used in combination as a policy instrument.

If this task looks formidable, the real needs are even more demanding: Consideration of the whole relevant legal system is an essential requisite for effective and efficient use of law as a tool of directed social change, but an inadequate one. The legal system being a subsystem of society, consideration of legal policy instruments in abstraction from other social policy instruments is misleading. Instead, the uses of law as a tool of social change must be considered within a broader series of possible policy instruments such as economic, educational, ecologic, and technological ones.

The relevant domains of policy instruments may be quite narrow when we deal with very limited policy objectives. But even when we take a relatively narrow objective, such as reducing court congestion, the relevant policy instruments are many, and a preferable mix may well include some from outside the legal system—such as insurance schemes to take care of some issues which today reach the courts. When we take the more significant social problems (such as, in the United States, race relations, public safety, drug use, pollution, and the like), the necessity to use law as a policy instrument only within a multiple mix of carefully considered social policy instruments should be quite convincing.

Our conclusions apply not only to the policy approach to law and social change, but to the behavioral approach, too. If we want to understand the operation of law as an independent variable in social change, we must study the social impact of changes in law within the context of the other components of the legal system and of other relevant policy variables. Since in no real case the requirement of "all other policy variables being static" is met, a complex multi-variable analysis seems essential for valid and reliable behavioral study of law and social change. Only such a methodology can provide the knowledge essential for supporting policy recommendations on how better to use law as a tool of directed social change (see Nagel, 1969).

LAW AND NORMATIVE POLICY ANALYSIS

A broad approach to the use of law as one policy instrument in combination with many others requires not only a new perspective on the relations between law, other legal-system policy instruments, and social policy instruments; it requires also a new methodology for designing and identifying preferable combinations of a multiplicity of policy instrument settings. This task is in all respects beyond the present and potential capacities of both jurisprudence and social sciences. Rather, it belongs to the emerging policy sciences (see Lasswell and McDougal, 1966) and especially to policy analysis which focuses on the stimulation of policy designs and identification of preferable policy alternatives.

Policy analysis constitutes an extension of systems analysis (see Churchman, 1968; Quade and Boucher, 1968) to complex policy issues which cannot be quantified and represented by exercizeable models (see Dror, 1970). Applied to the uses of law as a tool of directed social change, policy analysis (combined with knowledge on the substantive phenomena of law and social change, which must be supplied by behavioral study) is designed to provide systematic heuristic aid in dealing with the following interrelated issues (for important steps in the direction of a policy analysis approach to law and legal policy, see Nagel, 1966 and Mayo, 1964):

(a) Decision on main policy strategies in respect to risk, degrees of innovation, main goals, feasibility domain, and time perspective. Such explicit strategy decisions are essential for reducing the policy design and choice tasks to meaningful and manageable dimensions.

(b) Design of main policy alternatives, with different combinations of various changes in law with changes in other policy instruments.

(c) Prediction of probable consequences of main policy alternatives (with fast elimination of many of them if necessary so as to make further analysis easier) through novel methods such as social-legal experimentation and sequential decision-making on the uses of law.

(d) Examination of remaining main policy alternatives in terms of probable first, second, and third order consequences within a benefit-cost framework.

(e) Comparison of probable consequences in terms of value preferences with special attention to reduction of sensitivity to value differences and to impairment of other functions (including symbolic ones) of law.

(f) Presentation of policy analysis findings in a form conducive to political and executive decision-making through explicated judgment.

(g) Design of follow-up, evaluations, and policy-redesign instruments with special attention to the impact of the law instruments and to possibilities and costs of readjusting them.

Let me be clear: We do not yet know how to do good policy analysis, though much more is known than is used in actual policy-making. But the seven issues mentioned above must be faced in using law as a tool of directed social change and constitute parts of the basic framework for doing so. Therefore, policy analysis must constitute one of the foundations of a policy-oriented approach to law and social change.

APPLIED IMPLICATIONS

Our findings emphasize the necessity to base the study and practice of the use of law as a tool of directed social change on (1) a broad perspective of law as one of many policy instruments which must be used in combination, and (2) policy analysis as the methodology for identifying preferable combinations of such policy instruments. These findings have a number of applied implications, including in particular the following:

(a) As already mentioned, behavioral studies of the use of law as a tool of directed social change (and of law and social change in general) must be broadened to cover other relevant policy variables.

(b) Prescriptive study on the use of law as a tool of directed social change must be based on both a broad view of policy instruments and policy analysis methodology. This, in turn, requires:

(1) Mixed teams of lawyers, social scientists, and policy analysts to engage in relevant studies and prepare policy recommendations.

(2) Location of such teams at various points of the social guidance cluster, such as the legislature, the executive, special policy research organizations, and universities.

(3) Changes in various characteristics of the policy-making system so as to permit utilization of the work of such teams through a broader and more systematic approach to policy-making as a whole.[2]

(c) Essential for progress in the indicated directions is availability of highly qualified and motivated personnel for behavioral and prescriptive research on the uses of law as a tool of directed social change. This, in turn, requires:

(1) Changes in university training. In particular, law schools should become substantially policy-oriented and supply their interested students with basic knowledge in analytical approaches and in social sciences.[3] Also, the increasing number of special programs in policy science and public policy analysis should include the use of law as a policy instrument within these research and teaching programs. (See Dror, forthcoming.)

(2) Efforts to convey the necessary knowledge in analytical approaches to interested jurisprudence and social science scholars and the necessary knowledge in law and social sciences to interested analysts. This may, for instance, be done through summer institutes similar to the Social Science Research Council Summer Training Institutes which pioneered the rapprochment between social scientists and law.

Modern societies are more and more "active societies" (Etzioni, 1968). Law constitutes one of their sharper tools of direction—very useful when used correctly, very dangerous when utilized inapropriately. This explains the urgency of a new approach to the use of law as a tool of directed social change within a broad policy-making framework.

NOTES

1. For an excellent survey and discussion, see Stone (1966).

2. In many respects, improvements in the use of law as a tool of directed social change are impossible and perhaps dangerous, unless public policy-making as a whole is significantly improved. This in turn requires far-reaching progress in policy sciences. For a general theory of policy-making improvement, see Dror (1968). Stimulating in this context, though over-optimistic on the scope of science is Beutel (1957, 1968).

3. This proposal was first made in a modern form by Lasswell and McDougal (1943). Various attempts have been made in this direction, but with very limited success, especially because of neglect of analytical approaches. Contemporary student pressures and faculty interests seem to encourage new and promising efforts, such as the combined program in law and public policy at Harvard University and the proposed new program at Brandeis Law School.

REFERENCES

BEUTEL, F. K. (1965) Democracy or the Scientific Method in Law and Policy Making. Rio Piedras: Univ. of Puerto Rico.
––– (1957) Some Potentials of Experimental Jurisprudence as a New Branch of Social Science. Lincoln: Univ. of Nebraska Press.
CHURCHMAN, C. W. (1968) The Systems Approach. New York: Delacorte Press.
DROR, Y. (forthcoming) "Teaching of policy sciences: design for a doctorate university program." Social Sci. Information.
––– (1970) "Prolegomena to policy sciences." Policy Sci. 1, 1.
––– (1968) Public Policymaking Reexamined. San Francisco: Chandler.
ETZIONI, A. (1968) The Active Society: A Theory of Societal and Political Processes. New York: Free Press.
LASSWELL, H. D. and M. S. McDOUGAL (1966), "Jurisprudence in policy-oriented perspective." Univ. of Florida Law Rev. 19, 3: 486-513.
––– (1943) "Legal education and public policy: professional training in the public interest." Yale Law J. 52: 203-295.
MAYO, L. H. and E. M. JONES (1964) "Legal-policy decision process: alternative thinking and predictive function." George Washington Law Rev. 33, 1: 318-456.
NAGEL, S. (1969) The Legal Process from a Behavioral Perspective Homewood, Ill.: Dorsey.
––– (1966) "Optimizing legal policy." Univ. of Florida Law Rev. 18: 577-590.
QUADE, E. and W. I. BOUCHER, [eds.] (1968) Systems Analysis and Policy Planning. New York: American Elsevier.
STONE, J. (1966) Social Dimensions of Law and Justice. Palo Alto: Stanford Univ. Press.

Toward and Beyond a Theory of Supreme Court Impact

JAMES P. LEVINE
University of Oregon

THEODORE L. BECKER
New York University

The purpose of this paper is to explain why the Supreme Court has had limited effects on American society, to suggest some means by which the Court's influence can be increased, and to raise some questions about the proper role of social science in this endeavor.

REASONS FOR SUPREME COURT INEFFICACY

LOWER COURT AUTONOMY

It is often presumed that the hierarchical organization of the American judiciary centralizes much lawmaking authority within appellate courts and that trial courts generally defer to the Supreme Court in deciding cases of constitutional law. The operation of this role constraint on lower courts is illustrated by the Indiana Supreme Court's reaction to Henry Miller's *Tropic of Cancer*, which was involved in a local obscenity case. After expressing distaste for the book, the Indiana Court deferred to the authority of the superordinate court and reversed the conviction:

> Regardless of our personal opinion on this matter both as to the law and the facts, we are bound as judges of this Court, under the oath we took, to follow the Constitution of the United States, as interpreted by the Supreme Court of the United States, and that Court, in our opinion has determined the issue in this case.[1]

[83]

However, the "trickle-down" theory is at best just a very rough first approximation of reality. First of all, there is no solid evidence showing that most trial judges actually feel obliged to follow Supreme Court rulings if they are opposed to them. And unless the duty to comply is internalized, there are few means available to appellate courts to keep lower courts in line, since only a very small proportion of cases are ever appealed. Because the threat of reversal is fairly hollow, the trial judges can act independently with impunity.

Indeed, there are some data which suggest that lower courts frequently apply standards decidedly at variance with those articulated by the Supreme Court. For example, in Betts v. Brady,[2] (since overruled by Gideon v. Wainwright[3]), the Court ruled that defendants in noncapital cases were entitled to state-appointed counsel if special circumstances were present making it impossible for the defendant to represent himself adequately. However, in only 11 out of 139 state appellate cases concerning this issue were special circumstances found (Lewis, 1964: 151). In 1961, the Pennsylvania Supreme Court actually denied a plea for legal aid from an eighteen-year-old boy with an IQ of 59, equivalent to a mental age of nine.[4] Since Betts v. Brady was a landmark case, this smacks of outright defiance of the Supreme Court.

Many institutional features of the judicial system provide ample opportunity for inferior judges to legitimately ignore, modify, or evade high-level policy formulations (see Murphy, 1959). First, lower courts have the authority to make crucial findings of fact which can only be partially controlled by appellate courts. Second, since the fact constellations of any one case are never *exact* replicas of those of other cases, lower courts can often distinguish away alleged precedents ordained on high. Third, the verbiage of Supreme Court language can be manipulated, with favorable sentences elevated to the status of a "holding" which is binding and unfavorable words dismissed as "mere dicta." Fourth, state courts can often insulate themselves from Supreme Court review by grounding their decisions in state law. Thus, judges who want to be obstructive have adequate tools at their disposal.

Another impediment to Supreme Court efficacy is the very nature of most decisions. The Court is often either ambiguous or divided on policy matters, which gives lower courts encouragement to go their own way. Because compromise and negotiations are frequently necessary to obtain the support of most of the Justices (or even a bare majority) behind one opinion (Murphy, 1964: ch. 3), the resulting document is often beset with confusion providing lower courts with few guidelines to decide run-of-the-mill cases. If the Justices persevere and hold out for clearly written principles, the result is often a very split Court and the continuing possibility, of which lower courts are aware, that small changes of personnel will alter the balance on the Court and change its direction. There seems to be an inverse relation between the *clarity of holdings* and the *size of the Court majority*, so Justices must often choose between two routes to ineffectiveness. Chief Justice Earl Warren obtained unanimity in Brown v. Board of Education, but the price may have been the now infamously vague "all deliberate speed" mandate. On the other hand, when Warren in 1966 did spell out precise rules for police interrogations in Miranda v. Arizona,[5] only five Justices subscribed to his majority opinion (two of whom will be gone when the 1969 term convenes), and four Justices dissented. The Court, like others, may not be able to have its cake and eat it, too.

Even when a united Court is committed to some specific policy, the physical burden of handling a constantly increasing number of appeals often prevents them from periodically reinforcing this commitment and supervising implementation. The Court, for example, terminated its approval of the usage of the due process clause of the Fourteenth Amendment to invalidate economic legislation as early as the 1930s, but Paulsen (1950) has shown that lower courts continued to declare statutes unconstitutional on that basis for many years. Given its limited resources of time and manpower, the Court is simply unable to do much spotchecking of the lower courts except in issue areas of the highest priority.

Finally, linear trends are not characteristic of Supreme Court policymaking. The voting equality cases are atypical, what with the Court from 1962 to 1967 declaring 31 out of 32 instances of alleged malapportionment unconstitutional. Usually the Court exhibits occasional fluctuation or vacillation as it has done in the right to privacy cases. Such equivocation is probably seized upon by lower courts who oppose the general directions being taken and used to retard policy changes at the trial court level.

ELITE UNRESPONSIVENESS

Of more concern than lower court compliance with the Supreme Court is the conduct of presumably affected people who never get into the court at all. The real test of the Court's potency are the changes voluntarily initiated by those elites, public and private, whose activities are similar to those declared illegitimate by the Court. Due to the inertia which propels many organizations, there is a natural tendency to carry on established routines and disregard Court holdings that rock the boat. This is especially so where the Court strikes at central practices of the institution and where policy changes are perceived by those in control as being dysfunctional to primary objectives.

Thus, those who operate the criminal courts, which are usually oriented toward conviction (Blumberg, 1967), react negatively to court decisions extending defendants' rights, which would have the effect of turning a fairly efficient bureaucratic process into a time-consuming and nonproductive adversary system. Similarly, officials in the Selective Service System are unlikely to respond positively to judicial restrictions on draft board procedures which would curtail the rapid mobilization of military manpower. Indicative of this is General Hershey's recent disavowal of a federal court declaratory judgment ruling that it was illegal to speed up inductions of draft protestors.

Because no general announcements of policy are communicated to affected parties, it is quite frequent that authorities remain totally unaware of new responsibilities required of them and new norms governing their behavior. Barth found that district attorneys in Wisconsin are very ill-informed about current obscenity rulings (Barth, 1968), and Rabin's (1967) interviews with Selective Service personnel showed that they were oblivious to United States v. Seeger[6] which broadened the legitimate bases for conscientious objection. In a similar vein, Krislov (1968: 194) has pointed out that police training conferences pay virtually no attention whatsoever to development in civil liberties law.

There is frequently a high personal utility to willful noncompliance. Sometimes it is simply good politics to defy Court decisions, as the fortunes of George Wallace and Lester Maddox have dramatically demonstrated. In other cases the payoffs are even greater, as when the policeman in high crime districts obtains greater physical security by shortcutting the requirements of due process in enforcing the law. Muir's (1962: ch. 4) study of educators' reactions to the school prayer decisions points out a less tangible benefit resulting from resistance to the Court: the maintenance of social relationships and the approval of associates. In short, elites often see it in their own self-interest to turn their backs on the Court.

Since the judiciary really lacks the sanctions to coerce compliance, elites often see few risks ensuing from disobedience. Positive programs involving the allocation of considerable economic resources are often required to implement Court doctrines, and judicial enforcement machinery is largely limited to negative instruments such as injunctions and acquittals. Both the cost of litigations and the prerequisites of court utilization (e.g., establishing standing, showing a real case and controversy, actually violating a law) minimize the force of judicial controls. Moreover, the decentralized and uncoordinated nature of many institutions regulated by Supreme Court decisions (such as school boards, police departments, and welfare agencies) magnify the scope of the enforcement problem The attorneys general of the states supposedly have the authority to spur compliance, but Krislov (1959) and others have shown that they also often have political disincentives to act vigorously. To offend local norms and opinion can be political suicide.

The beneficiaries of Supreme Court policies are often either ill-equipped or unwilling to pressure elites to comply: It is often insular minorities who are supported by the Court, and they lack the resources —the funds, personnel, organization, and information—to mount a cause at the local level. The poor are hardly in a position to push for their constitutional rights to equal governmental treatment.

Also, the cost of pushing compliance usually outweighs the limited satisfaction of having one's interest vindicated. Parents may be irritated by Bible-reading in their children's classrooms, and public employees may be troubled by compulsory loyalty oaths, but the intensity of their grievances is insufficient to motivate them to act. For criminal defendants, the price of insisting on the right to appointed counsel may very well be harsher treatment by the court and stiffer sentences. It is normal for persons to try to maximize their utilities, and fighting for constitutional rights is often just not worthwhile.

Consequently, the deck is rather stacked against widespread voluntary implementation of Supreme Court policies. Institutions such as Congress, with its control over the public fisc, and the executive, with its massive bureaucracy, are in a far better postition to promote social change on more than a token basis. For example, it was not until the United States Commissioner of Education started a systematic campaign to enforce the Federal Aid to Education Act of 1965, which prohibited funding of segregated schools, that any serious progress was made toward desegregation of schools in the deep South. Without political action in other quarters, the hands of the Supreme Court are likely to be tied and the status quo ante will probably remain.

PUBLIC UNAWARENESS

Although the Supreme Court has the inherent capacity to mold its decisions into powerful political symbols, the empirical evidence on symbolic effects of decisions is still meager. Hyman and Sheatsley

(1964) analyzed survey data on changes in attitudes toward desegregation from 1942 to 1964 and concluded that the Brown decision had radically accelerated the shift towards acceptance of desegregation. More recently Dolbeare (1969: 185-187) found that the "halo effect" caused by the Supreme Court's virtuous image caused people to applaud the Court's banning of public school prayers, even though they had previously approved of schoolhouse religion. Since political leaders do respond to public moods and sentiments, these kinds of consequences can be important in the formation of public policy.   However, there is a missing link in the above line of argument: the communication processes between the Court and the public. Judicial symbols must be widely diffused to be effective, and the findings of survey research are beginning to unfold massive public ignorance of Supreme Court decisions (Dolbeare, 1967). News coverage of the Court is generally sketchy and frequently either misunderstood or distorted, with major decisions often relegated to back pages or summarized in a couple of column inches (for all but assiduous and devoted readers of the *New York Times*. See Newland, 1964). If the Court is to be a catalyst of major social change, it must reach beyond the legal community (which remains largely untouched anyway) and into the general community.

INCREASING THE SUPREME COURT'S IMPACT

To increase the Court's impact, some traditional practices should be abandoned as quickly as possible while new approaches and procedures are adopted and applied—with imagination, flexibility, and boldness. Since the social isolation treasured by most of the Justices mutes the Court's voice in national politics, we urge, as a start, that the Court give up this haughty posture and begin making serious attempts to relate to the American public.

Some innovations might necessitate legislative action, but others could be instituted by the Court itself, thereby obviating resort to the booby-trapped trail through the legislative obstacle course called Congress. Let us take a candid look at how the Court clues us all in on what it has decided in camera. Its "streamlined" method is rooted in practices developed under Forefather John Jay, as modified by that other great modernist, Forefather John Marshall, as well as by other radical proceduralists. Of course these jurisprudential giants of yesteryear were acquainted, to a degree, with the political system as it existed in their heyday. But need we emphasize that the times, they have a-changed? In today's world, the medium is the message, and the medium that the Court chooses to pass its word is drab, dreary, and—to be blunt—a drag. Verbatim reading of opinions by the Justices to handfuls of court observers and the doling out of advance sheets to lawyers and libraries are that medium. Small wonder that so few get the message!

We are certain that a multitude of arguments, mostly sunk in tradition, can be mustered to applaud this musty arrangement. However, if we may be so brash, as political scientists currently interested in a more effective Court, we would suggest a vast array of changes in the props of the setting on opinion day. For one thing, there is surely no reasons, in this, the age of McLuhan, to categorically exclude television from the court chambers. In our era of mass communications, it is almost anachronistic that the Court has shunned the tube for as long as it has. We are well aware, of course, that if the Justices were to perform before the cameras as they now do in the flesh, there is little doubt that their Nielsen ratings would set record lows. Justice Black's ponderous performance on a recent network television interview does nothing to dispel this suspicion.

But can there be any question about the fact that one reason the Court receives so little popular support for important decisions is that the public simply does not comprehend what the Court has said and why the Justices believe their view to be proper? Since television networks donate free time to the President to express his views in news conferences and through prepared speeches, it would seem that they could be convinced (or forced by law) to open their facilities, once a month, perhaps, to the Court for a professionally designed program describing and dramatizing what it is that the Court has decided and spelling out the justifications for its policies.

True, this might be nudging the judiciary into the realm of theatrics. But so what? And true, this might compel the Court to employ a staff that would include television or movie directors, actors, and technicians, in order to produce short vignettes about what the Court finds offensive in the actions of some officials and what the scope of its rulings really are. In doing this, the Court will be assuming one of its basic responsibilities; it will be taking a direct hand in creating an illuminating presentation that could truly educate the public on constitutional politics. Years ago, Eugene Rostow (1952: 203) characterized the Justices as "teachers in a vital national seminar" about fundamental political principles, but it is a sad fact that few Americans are enrolled in the course. The Court has ignored its pedagogical functions and has passed the buck to woefully inadequate sources of information, such as harried newspaper reporters, copy editors, and headline writers pressured by deadlines into frequently misinterpreting and malinterpreting.

It is sometimes written that the Presidency became the political power into which it has evolved as the President became aware of the role of mass media in gaining grassroots support. FDR'S fireside chats were a significant device that aided President Roosevelt in consolidating the coalition so essential to his continuation in office through four elections. Several Presidents since have managed to use television, in particular, to their own political advantage so as to maximize the chances for getting favored policies accepted by large segments of the citizenry. The Court's refusal to admit this to itself and its continued abhorrence of this most significant of media may well undermine its remaining vestiges of influence. One can hardly understand or respect even the most eloquent of orators if he speaks only into a paper bag: Only the orator hears a resonance of the beautiful rhetoric; others hear muffled sounds.

Aside from recognizing this failing, there are changes in staffing that the Justices should consider. After all, it is rather absurd to pretend that the only help the Court needs is that of its law clerks and its secretarial and administrative staffs. Neither these people nor the Justices themselves qualify as experts in political analysis or in the arts of public relations and political pressure. How long must we wait until the common knowledge among us that the Court is a political institution is translated into meaningful reforms in how the Court acts in the political system?

For instance, it is well known that the Court frequently runs into stiff opposition from Congress. There have been many studies that detail the hatred and defiance among members of the Senate and the House of Representatives that the Court has triggered by some of its most recent decisions (see, for example, Beaney and Beiser, 1964; Nagel, 1965). But what is worse still is that the Court is frequently misunderstood by even its staunchest supporters who, on the basis of the idle conjecture and often amateurish speculation, bear the onerous burden of communicating accurately to their legislative colleagues the precise holding of the Court and the political and legal reasons behind the Court's decision. What possible benefit can be gained in allowing this fumbling and groping to continue? Whom are we kidding? Whom is the Court fooling? Surely the Congress is not (comprised): of a naive clique of legal positivists who believe en masse that the Court *finds* the law a la Lord Coke. They recognize that a host of extra legal factors influence the Court's decision as well as we do. Why, then, don't we do for the Court that which we have done for administrative agencies (like the Pentagon) and furnish the Court with a group of political scientists, lobbyists, and public relations men to plead its case before Congress? These men could also assist the Court in moulding and writing opinions that would hold down potential irritation levels of Congress (and the President) thus enhancing the chances of maximum compliance.

As to the political scientists on an expanded Supreme Court staff, their role would be far more than simply figuring out political ploys and tactics on the Hill. Indeed, the time has come (if not gone) when the Court must officially recognize the need for developing a large store of data on success and failure in implementing its announced law at all levels of government. It would seem to be the proper place, in our scheme of things, to sponsor these studies through the Court itself. As the first section of this paper shows clearly enough, political scientists are already deeply committed to a search into what conditions foster (or undermine) compliance with Supreme Court decisions. As this area of study grows, and as theory begins to take shape, it would seem the height of folly for the Court to dwell in ignorance of the findings as well as of expert advice from political scientists interested in a more effective Supreme Court.

WITHDRAWING SCIENTIFIC SUPPORT

This leads us into the final point we wish to make in this paper. It is a difficult one, and one that plunges us deeply into thorny dilemmas about the appropriate role of empirical scientists assisting those who hold the reins of power.

We have been reminded of late of the naivete of many nuclear physicists, in the early and mid-forties, concerning the uses to which their knowledge and expertise would be put by our government. This blindness has been dramatized by a play entitled *In The Matter of J. Robert Oppenheimer* (presented at New York City Lincoln Center's Vivian Beaumont Threatre during the 1968-1969 season). According to the testimony given at Oppenheimer's security hearing, many of these scientists refused to believe that the bomb would actually be used against the Japanese people. This belief was firm enough to resist change despite the fact that the military had several of these very same scientists (including Oppenheimer) working on problems of heat and blast effects on a variety of Japanese cities!

Transposed to studies of the Supreme Court, the problem presents itself thusly: we must be alert constantly to future changes in our political system and its processes and consciously determine the point at which we should withdraw scientific support of governmental policies once we believe them to be inimical to political values that we cherish. To fail to see this as a problem would be immoral and irresponsible.

It is easy for many of us who consider ourselves to be a shade of liberal (or even a hue of conservative) to rail at the mosaic of non-compliance with Supreme Court decisions. After all, the Supreme Court is the duly constituted final arbiter of a wide variety of federal and constitutional questions and issues. When it speaks, its words are the *supreme law* of the land. And law must be obeyed. Therefore, as scientists, we can plunge in without any reluctance and treat the malady of defiance. Right? Wrong.

That was the error of the nuclear physicists who trotted gallantly out in quest of the secret of the atomic bomb. But, as many of them discovered later, and as many other scientists who have been employed by the American military-industrial complex have learned more recently, they were utilized to achieve ends that they came to consider evil, unjust and wrong. At some earlier point, they may have had a bargaining position that might have allowed them, as citizens—with power (scientific knowledge)—to influence processes and policies. But they were dazzled by a golden ideological haze that convinced them that American power could only be used for good. Only at a point too far removed, and after the fact, did they come to their normative senses. We must begin to think about this problem now, in all areas of the study of government and politics, and that would certainly include our potential use to the Supreme Court as political scientists and as political advisors.

We do not wish to belabour this point, but there is a thick and durable smog of nonsense that cloaks the actual functioning of the Supreme Court of the United States. The basic function of the Court is surely not the one we find so consistently uttered by much of the political-legal community in this day and age. For liberals, all too often, the Court is pictured as some eternal fortress, of sorts, against encroachments on the democratic process and on individual liberties. To one degree of another, the Court is seen by prominent experts as being an important factor in expanding our freedoms and in developing legal guidelines for expanding our democratic base. And, of course, in a legal sense, and to some degree of political reality, it has had this function of late on the American scene. Our point is that this is more an accident of history and a result of particular personnel than it is an inherent function of the Supreme Court.[7]

Who in their right minds could believe that the United States Supreme Court, or any other high court for that matter, is anything other than an *un*democratic institution? Despite rationales to the contrary we have no serious structural democratic checks by the populace directly as they exist in Australia and Japan. Of course our Court's judges, as an enlightened and benevolent aristocracy, have had strong democratic and liberal ideals and thus have made decisions that are *pro*-democratic and *anti*-police state. But, and this is critical, there is no guarantee that such a status-quo-oriented, elite-staffed institution will continue to decide as it has in the last decade or so. We must remember that the same Court produced the Dred Scott Decision.[8]

Suppose, for example, President Nixon and his successor—say, a President Agnew—get another twelve years in the White House. Suppose they manage to select an overwhelming number of highly reactionary justices. Suppose the court of Chief Justice Warren Earl Burger reverses precedents (with some relish) and tries to implement a personal policy preference of seriously curtailing the protections of the Fifth Amendment. Suppose, even, that the Supreme Court becomes more police-state oriented than many high police administrators and that the latter, contrary to the Court's mandates, devise ingenious plans for evasion, avoidance, and defiance? Thus we might find career bureaucrats trying to sabotage what some people fear as being imminent on the horizon, that is, a drastic "turn to the right." What then for those among us who would be working out a theory on the impact of the Supreme Court? Should we continue to work it out? Should we continue to advise on how the Court can be most effective? The problem that we must ponder is again to set forth specific criteria by which changes in our system and its process and policies should force us to withdraw scientific support, *as a profession*!

This should be debated in our classrooms, in our literature, and at our conventions—local and national. It would be tragic for social scientists to ignore this issue much the same as it was overlooked by the nuclear physicists in the forties and the entire scientific community in the fifties and sixties. After all, we have their lesson to learn from and we are, or should be *political* scientists.

CONCLUSION

In an age of almost incomprehensibly rapid changes, institutions which fail to keep pace are bound for oblivion. Miller's (1968: ch. 6) ominous predictions about the coming "desuetude" of the Supreme Court may prove to be correct unless the Court adjusts its strategies and tactics. Theodore Roosevelt is alleged to have urged nations seeking world power to speak softly and carry a big stick. To which we add, those who lack big sticks, like the United States Supreme Court, had better learn to yell loudly, plead fervidly, and act shrewdly. The Court's strength is in its symbols; it should make the best of them.

Lest we conclude on a self-righteous and self-assured note, it must be admitted that we of the academy will take *some* of the blame for the tragically wide gulf between the ideals of constitutional doctrine and the reality of political life. Having criticized the Supreme Court for blindly staggering in the dark and cloistering itself inside the marble palace, we must also point a guilty finger at the discipline of political science for failing to light the way and for taking refuge in the ivory tower. Both our research and our teaching have only very recently been directed to the empirical study of institutional practices and their social consequences, which is one area where we *ourselves* can aspire to make a political impact.

Finally, now that increasing attempts are being made to devise more refined theory and collect better data on the impact of the Supreme Court, let us not make the grievous error of being indifferent to the real danger of having our knowledge used for malevolent purposes. If and when the day should come that the Supreme Court becomes repressive, inhumane, and unjust in its policy-making, we may have a political obligation to confound their efforts by quashing our inquiries and withdrawing our counsel. It is not too early to ponder these disturbing possibilities and perplexing dilemmas; 1984 is only fifteen years away.

NOTES

1. Cuffel v. State, 215 N.E. 2d 36 (Indiana, 1966).
2. 316 U.S. 455 (1942).
3. 372 U.S. 335 (1963).
4. Commonwealth ex rel. Simon v. Maroney, 405 Pa. 562 (1961).
5. 384 U.S. 436 (1966).
6. 380 U.S. 163 (1965).
7. For the fullest argument along these lines, see Becker (1969: ch. 5). A more cursory treatment of this point can be found in Becker (1967).
8. Dred Scott v. Sanford, 19 Howard (U.S.) 393 (1857).

REFERENCES

BARTH, T. (1968) "Perception and acceptance of Supreme Court decisions at the state and local level." J. of Public Law 17: 308-350.

BEANEY, W. M. and E. N. BEISER (1964) "Prayer and politics: the impact of Engel and Schempp on the political process." J. of Public Law 13: 475-503.

BECKER, T. L. (1969) Comparative Judicial Politics. Chicago: Rand-McNally.

――― (1967) "Judicial structure and its political functioning in society." J. of Politics 29: 302-331.

BLUMBERG, A. (1967) Criminal Justice. Chicago: Quadrangle.

DOLBEARE, K. (1969) "The Supreme Court and the states: from abstract doctrine to local behavioral conformity," in T. Becker (ed.) The Impact of Supreme Court Decisions. New York: Oxford Univ. Press.

――― (1967) "The public views the Supreme Court," pp. 194-212 in H. Jacob (ed.) Law, Politics, and the Federal Courts. Boston: Little, Brown.

HYMAN, H. and P. SHEATSLEY (1964) "Attitudes toward desegregation." Scientific Amer. 211: 16-23.

KRISLOV, S. (1968) The Supreme Court and Political Freedom. New York: Free Press.

――― (1959) "Constituency versus constitutionalism: the desegregation issue and the tensions and aspirations of Southern attorneys general." Midwest J. of Pol. Sci. 3: 75-92.

LEWIS, A. (1964) Gideon's Trumpet. New York: Vantage.

MILLER, A. (1968) The Supreme Court and American Capitalism. New York: Free Press.

MUIR, W. (1962) Prayer in the Public Schools. Chicago: Univ. of Chicago Press.

MURPHY, W. (1964) Elements of Judicial Strategy. Chicago: Univ. of Chicago Press.

――― (1959) "Lower court checks on Supreme Court power." Amer. Pol. Sci. Rev. 53 (December): 1017-1031.

NAGEL, S. (1965) "Court-curbing periods in American history." Vanderbilt Law Rev. 18 (June): 925-944.

NEWLAND, C. (1964) "Press coverage of the United States supreme court." Western Pol. Q. 17 (March): 15-36.

PAULSEN, M. (1950) "The persistence of substantive due process in the states." Minnesota Law Rev. 34 (January): 91-118.

RABIN, R. (1967) "Do you believe in a supreme being—the administration of the conscientious objector exemption." Wisconsin Law Rev.: 642-684.

ROSTOW, E. (1952) "The democratic character of judicial review." Harvard Law Rev. 66 (December).

Law and Social Change in Marxist Africa

JOHN N. HAZARD
Columbia University

RELEVANT MARXIST LEGAL BELIEFS

Marxist-oriented leaders believe that social change can be manipulated through management of economic resources; that a relative few with understanding of the process can and must provide direction, and that law is a primary instrument of implementation. No Marxist ignores the potential for resistance in a population imbued with traditional values and guided by hoary custom, but he has faith in his ability to overcome these brakes upon what he believes to be progress. The history of states led by Marxists, of whatever degree of acceptance of the faith and on whatever continent, is written in the struggle between a determined leadership and a recalcitrant people.

This is not to say that there is uniformity of evolution. Many variations occur as one or another leader exerts the influence of his personality upon the process. Some, like Joseph Stalin, are prepared to press for swift change while making minimal concessions to the sluggish crowd, while others, like Alexander Dubček of Czechoslavakia, will bend to pressures from citizens who play upon their leader's more firmly rooted conviction of the priority to be given humanistic values.

Sub-Saharan Africa provides no exception to the general rule. Some of its Marxist-oriented leaders, like Modibo Keita of Mali, have pressed so hard for reform that they have been toppled by the resistance of a militantly dissatisfied people. Others, like Lépold Sédar Senghor of Sénégal, have taken an easier course, making concessions in such number as to cause more orthodox Marxists to doubt their ability to ultimately achieve the classless society they espouse.

Perhaps the sun is now setting on those Africans who came to power dreaming of quick social change through Marxist-oriented manipulation. The charismatic leaders are falling one by one under the pressures of military men, supported—or at least unopposed—by peoples fatigued by forced draft campaigns showing little return for the sacrifices demanded.

But even as the first-generation leadership is pushed aside, a residue of Marxism remains. It is symptomatic that the revolutionary Army lieutenants of Mali who delivered their president to prison in November 1968 found it necessary to woo trade union support by acquiescing in continuation of the policy of state ownership of the basic means of industrial production. Marxist-inspired fear that private owners would impede nonexploitive social change had been so firmly implanted as to defy retreat. Only the villagers who had been scarcely touched by Marxist indoctrination hastened to push aside Keita's village system to return to traditional ways of tilling the land.

GENERAL IMPACT OF MARXIST LEGAL THOUGHT IN AFRICA

Americans carry on a great debate over the influence of Marxist thought in Africa (African Law Studies, 1969: 45-102). Some believe that the imperatives of development in impoverished societies dictate state investment, economic planning, organization of farmers into co-operatives, and creation of strong leadership functioning without threat of disruptive opposition. This view suggests that those phenomena of African development could have emerged spontaneously if Marx had never lived and if there had been no Soviet model. Pragmatists could not have escaped moving in the direction that has been taken.

While the argument of spontaneity has attraction, particularly when read in light of Vernadsky's (1947: 4) assertion that early Germanic and Slavic law indicated similarities not because of conscious copying but because of similarities in general conditions of life, in social organization, and in tribal mentality, it overlooks a primary factor. It ignores the training and early experience of many French-speaking charismatic leaders who studied Marx and associated closely with members of the French Communist Party, either directly or through the French trade unions.

No biographer of Sékou Touré, Lépold Sédar Senghor, or Modibo Keita can minimize the Marxist component in their personal evolution. The fact that only Keita espoused Marxian socialism as the "universal truth" that governed his course is no proof that Marxist thought has been uninfluential elsewhere. Senghor (1964) is prepared to mix Teilhard de Chardin with Marx to create the basis for a new African concept call négritude, but there is no neglect of respect for Marx's analysis of the course of history. The difference between Senghor and Stalin is the emphasis upon the early Marx, upon humanism, but both anticipate achievement of the classless society without capitalists.

Touré (1966), likewise, although denying that his "non-capitalist way" will necessarily lead to communism, believes that property ownership is the key to social control and that he can achieve the classless society. He, like Keita and Senghor, espouses Marxism as a reality and a source of inspiration, although he does not require precise copying of the Soviet experience.

American and English scholars are not justified in concluding from their own experience that creeds taught by schoolmasters play no part in French-speaking Africa. French fondness for doctrine runs deep, and education in creeds to guide social development has penetrated deeply into the minds of men of French education, even though they improvise in detail to meet the needs of their special societies.

SPECIFIC IMPACTS OF MARXIST
LEGAL THOUGHT IN AFRICA

OWNERSHIP IN INDUSTRY AND AGRICULTURE

Examination of these details will demonstrate the extent to which Marxist thought has played a part in Africa. The economies of Sénégal, Guinea and Mali are divided into public and private sectors as they were in Lenin's Russia during the period of the New Economic Policy. The division results not only from convenience in channelling development funds into areas thought in need of speedy social change but also for political reasons springing from Marxist thought. Senghor, Touré, and Keita distrust private owners of great productive wealth, whether foreigners or Africans. While this hostility might be traced to nationalist revulsion against the great exploiting French companies of the past, this cannot be the sole explanation. The avowed aim is to prevent the emergence of a capitalist class among Africans. The three leaders fear, in keeping with Marxist thought, that African capitalists would oppose planning in the interest of the community as a whole, out of a desire for personal aggrandizement. The Marxist-oriented leaders hope to minimize opposition from pressure groups opposing socialistically-oriented schemes for development.

Compromise has become necessary, but not exceeding the limits established by Lenin for Russia in 1922. Lenin permitted the return to private owners or the leasing to new entrepreneurs of enterprises nationalized during the period of militant communism between 1917 and 1920. Touré, in Guinea, will not even go that far. He wants no private activity except in the artisan's workshop. Keita was similarly restrictive. Only Senghor has seen fit to permit existing private enterprises to remain, but these were never numerous, except for merchants. Touré will not even tolerate merchants and has declared war on them, excluding them from his governing party. Senghor tolerates the merchants as a palliative to a people inclined to judge prosperity by what they see in the stores, but he anticipates the day when the state can buy out the capitalists and create the classless society.

For the farmers the programs of Keita, Touré, and Senghor have been far less ambitious than those introduced in the industrial sector, but they were Marxist in conception. None of the three leaders were faced on assuming their presidencies with Lenin's problem of land-lordism. Old French West Africa had found great plantations out of the question. The arid land, watered only during a rainy season, could produce only peanuts. Secondly, there was no western-type ownership of land. Villagers tilled it on assignment by chiefs to individual families, although in some areas part of the village land was retained for communal use. Villagers sold their produce to usurious middleman, who in turn delivered it to great French import-export firms which marketed the crops abroad. To the Marxist, there were in this commercial relationship two evil actors, the middlemen and the French exporters. He determined to eliminate both.

To effectuate their aims, the three Presidents introduced policies centered upon the introduction of cooperatives to take the form first of marketing cooperatives and later of producing units. Touré disclosed his scheme in a basic statute (August 9, 1960) creating three stages of development from simple marketing cooperatives to a form reminiscent of the Soviet collective farm. Senghor took only the first step, establishing a model (May 20, 1960) and creating an Office of Animation to aid villagers in organizing their marketing cooperative. Sales were to be to a state corporation charged with marketing the crops abroad. Keita tried to utilize for Marxist purposes the tribal custom of communal fields, requiring that they be enlarged annually from virgin land and from private plots, and urging his villagers to spend increasing amounts of time on them (1966: 4).

As to land ownership, only Senghor paralleled Lenin in nationalizing the bulk of it (June 17, 1964), although his reasons were not Lenin's. He felt the need to provide plots for industry and modern farms without fear of tribal claims (Aurillac, 1962: 99). Keita and Touré preferred to leave land tenure as it was under the French: registered in urban localities as in France, and distributed in accordance with tribal custom in the villages. Under their system, when transfers to modern usage became necessary, an administrative board heard claims and paid compensation.

Both Keita and Touré followed Senghor's scheme to exclude the French import-export corporation by creating monopoly state corporations to sell the produce abroad and to import basic commodities.

ECONOMIC PLANNING

Second to ownership on the Marxist agenda comes economic planning. Modern Marxists do not debate whether Marx envisioned it; they simply consider it essential to development and the implication of his system of man's control over his destiny. The Africans differ in planning from their Eastern European counterparts only because of the limitations created by the fact that they inherited almost no industry, their public sectors are miniscule, and their people are very far from understanding what planning discipline requires.

Under such circumstances, African planning is only a pale shadow of its Eastern European counterparts. Nevertheless, it exists. Each of the three Presidents: (1) created planning bodies charged with establishing priorities for development; (2) set up a licensing procedure to govern foreigners wishing to invest; and (3) also set up the state treasuries. Keita and Touré thought control of credit necessary to ensure enforcement. Touré abolished all foreign banks, and Keita, all but one. Both Presidents cut the link between their currencies and the French franc. Only Senghor perceived a continuing economic advantage in tapping French capital through existing French banks and in maintaining a currency convertible into francs.

Keita had to reverse himself not long before he was ousted, for he could not maintain the stability of his currency. He had to reestablish his link with the franc in 1967, but he did so with the utmost caution. He tightened the reins of control by suspension of sessions of the National Assembly and even altered the structure of his political party to permit himself to rule with only a very narrow group of associates.

CODE AND COURT REFORM

Having attacked the capitalist enemy on the economic front from which power was presumed to flow, the three Presidents turned to restructuring society by revision of codes of law: criminal, civil, procedural, and family. Speed seems to have been of lower priority than in attacking the major sources of power. Perhaps also the leaders considered that personal relationships resting on custom and religion cannot be manipulated as quickly as industrial and commercial ownership, for which Africans had very little concern. Whatever the reasons, the record shows that none of the three Presidents took the bold step taken by Lenin in 1917 in abrogating the old codes and substituting "revolutionary consciousness" as the source of law. The African Marxists chose to favor continuity, and it was some years before new codes were promulgated.

The major problem was perceived to be the relationship between a program of guided social change and customary law. The French had adopted a policy of permitting the tribes to administer their customary law through Justices of the Peace and their Islamic law through *cadis*. Both Touré and Keita decided that the special courts would have to close, and they threw all cases into the new unified system of general courts (October 15, 1958 and May 15, 1961, respectively). They made provision, however, for continued use of customary law where applicable by providing for the seating of specialists in this law from the tribes in the general court as legal advisors. Senghor chose a less radical departure from the past, continuing the old special courts but subject to appeal to a single Supreme Court (M'Baye, 1964).

CRIMINAL LAW

The criminal codes were the first in the substantive field to be replaced. When they appeared, they showed none of the features characteristic of codes of the Soviet republics. The Presidents and their legal advisors had opted for stability of law by continuing French attitudes. Analogy was rejected in spite of its popularization during Stalin's time. Judges had to find an article of the code applicable to an offense. They could not exercise their initiative as in Stalin's Soviet Union to punish whatever seemed dangerous to them regardless of whether it had been specifically defined as criminal.

Likewise, the African codes rejected the Soviet type chapter on "counterrevolutionary crime," and there was no crime vaguely defined as "crime against the proletariat." There were no chapters on "economic crime" until Touré introduced them in 1964 and incorporated them in his criminal code of 1965 to reflect his antagonism to merchants and embezzelers of public funds (Criminal Code Articles 361 and 365). Keita introduced into his 1961 criminal code the crime of vagabondage with a Marxist-sounding preamble declaring that "Labor is the duty of every

Malian," and in 1964 he chose to use the words "economic crimes" to cover fraud, contraband, and other voluntary and premeditated actions against economic, financial, and banking institutions (February 1, 1964).

Even with this movement in the direction of specially defined economic crime, there was no copying of Soviet models, where economic crime is punishable by death. African Marxists have rejected capital punishment, for anything except murder or treason, as violating the African humanistic value system.

FAMILY LAW

Customary and Islamic law had exercised their greatest influence on domestic relations over the centuries, and all three Presidents have sponsored the drafting of new family codes. Polygamy has been attacked by all, as has the giving of gifts so great as to impoverish households. Yet, on both counts, the attack has been limited. Polygamy was to be limited through a system of voluntary restraint controlled through marriage contracts. If the prospective spouses agreed upon a mongamous family, the state would enforce the contract by prosecution for bigamy unless the parties amended the contract. Not until 1968 did Touré abolish polygamy entirely.

The giving of gifts at the time of marriage or the giving of feasts at baptism and marriage had impoverished many African families. The new codes sought to control the excesses by establishing limits on the amounts of the gifts and on the expenditures for feasts. Guinea strengthened the prohibitions by requiring that local Party representatives participate in the planning of feasts.

Marriage was secularized by all three Presidents, and the arrangement of marriage by parents was prohibited. While Marxists would applaud such measures and have introduced them into the Soviet codes, the model for Africans has probably been France, rather than Eastern Europe. No Marxist explanations are given by Africans for amendment of family law.

PUBLIC LAW

In public law, the three Presidents chose to ignore the USSR's experience with working-class "soviets" sharing legislative and administrative authority. The French structure of government was maintained almost intact, except for an effort to replace local chiefs in the villages with men attuned to modern ideas. The major innovation in public law was the creation of the monopoly political party, which Senghor prefers to call the "dominant" party. Some see these parties as structured on the model of the French communist party, but there are some sharp departures from Lenin's concept. Most notably, none of the three ruling parties is seen as composing only an elite. All three Presidents permit any who wish to enter, although Touré excluded merchants after beginning his merchant war, and Keita tried to limit membership when his power began to totter.

Second, the parties depart from the communist model in their failure to maintain strict discipline, in spite of clauses providing for the existence of "democratic centralism." Indeed, it was for lack of party discipline that Keita was unable to rally his party behind him in 1968, and his party was the first institution to disintegrate after his arrest.

Some astute specialists on West Africa had foreseen such a possibility. Wallerstein had begun to speak of the decline of the single party in 1966 (1966). Senghor even admitted in an interview in 1964 that his power rested more on his position as President of the Republic than on his role as Secretary General of his party, because in his constitutional capacity he commanded the Army.

The major deviation from Marxist-Leninist patterns in Marxist Africa has, consequently, been in the character of the monopoly parties. Although they have been declared "vanguard" in emulation of Lenin, they have failed to achieve this role. They have been neither elite nor disciplined.

THE FUTURE OF MARXIST THOUGHT IN
AFRICAN LAW AND SOCIAL CHANGE

Keita's ouster in 1968 was only the dramatic moment marking the decline of Marxist influence in that part of Africa where it had started to show great promise when Touré voted "No" in the French referendum. Senghor had already dulled the sharp edges of his Marxist base, although leaving intact his strong position against the creation of African capitalists. Touré alone adhered firmly to his original position and his law, although professing no further interest in the very long-range future and Marxism's traditional promise of communism without state compulsion. Many believe that his people will not much longer enforce his policy of austerity.

Even the Soviet Marxists have become disappointed with the situation, seeing in West Africa today not communism in its early stages but "the non-capitalist way" (Academy of Sciences, 1967). Yet they still profess hope that the tide may flow again in the direction of what they consider salvation for man. They continue to provide economic and technical aid and to train hundreds of young West Africans in their Universities in the Soviet political and legal model. Their stance seems to be not abandonment but watchful waiting with confidence that if they assist in producing wealth in this impoverished area, the flow of history as Marx found it cannot but be resumed under the pressure of an increasing working class and under leadership of men whom know how to manipulate the pressures. Historical materialists have faith in their discipline, which makes unnecessary adherence to a time schedule to prove its validity.

Had the Soviet Union been able to pump into West African economies massive aid of the kind the Marxist-oriented leaders requested, the current malaise might have been avoided. The base for Marxist-type social change had been laid in the law. But the law is not enough to create conditions for breakthrough. There must be resources, both material and human, and these were lacking in qualities sufficient to create conditions acceptable to peoples led to expect almost instant change after independence and of no mind to wait out a long period of austerity and self-sacrifice, in whatever name it was justified.

REFERENCES

Academy of Sciences USSR (1967) The Non-Capitalist Way of Development of African Countries. Moscow: Nauka [in Russian].

African Law Studies (1969) Preliminary Issue. New York: African Law Center, Columbia University.

AURILLAC, M. (1962) "Les aspects juridiques du socialisme sénégalais." Annales Africaines 1: 93.

Journal Officiel de la République de Guinée (1960) Law on cooperatives. No. 18 (August 9): 218.

——— (1958) Judiciary act. No. 2 (October 15): 15.

Journal Officiel de la République du Mali (1964) Law on economic crimes. No. 162 (February 1): 91.

——— (1961) Judiciary act. No. 90 (May 15): 1.

Journal Officiel de la République du Sénégal (1964) Law on land nationalization. (June 17): 905.

——— (1960) Law on cooperatives. No. 18 (August 9): 218.

KEITA, M. (1966) "Discours au sixiéme anniversaire." L'Essor (September 26): 4.

M'BAYE, K. (1964) L'Organisation Judiciaire au Sénégal. Dakar (mimeo).

SENGHOR, L. S. (1964) on African Socialism (M. Cook, trans.). New York: Frederick A. Praeger.

TOURE, A. S. (1966) L'Afrique et la Révolution. Conakry.

VERNADSKY, G. (1947) Medieval Russian Laws. New York: Columbia Univ. Press.

WALLERSTEIN, E. (1966) "The decline of the party in single-party African states," pp. 201-214 in J. LaPalombara and M. Weiner (eds.) Political Parties and Political Development. Princeton: Princeton Univ. Press.

Science Challenges Law

Some Interactions Between Scientific and Legal Changes

ARTHUR SELWYN MILLER
George Washington University

That the scientific revolution is posing critical problems to traditional conceptions of law and of the legal system is fast becoming one of the truisms of the day. For science and its handmaiden, technology, not only mean change—awesome and rapid almost beyond measure—they have also brought about the means by which change can be managed. For the first time in human history, man now has the capability to invent the future (Schon, 1967). As Bell (1967) puts it, "Perhaps the most important social change of our time is the emergence of a process of direct and deliberate contrivance of change itself."

The development comes at a time when it is being increasingly recognized that, as Nagel (1961) has said, there is an "absence of well-established and generally accredited theories of social change." Our knowledge is primitive. Hence, any statements about the interaction of scientific and legal change are at best tentative formulations, offered to suggest possible avenues of needed research rather than definitive answers.

Law, in its historical sense, was considered to be a series of "thou shall nots," or, as Holmes once said, it is necessary to look upon law through the eyes of the "bad man"—he who asks what sanctions will be invoked if he acts in a certain way. That conception is now seen to state a half-truth at best; Hart (1961) has demonstrated that it is more necessary to see law through the eyes of the "good man" in order to perceive its role in society. One should go even further than that: Historical law was not only interdictory in nature, it was also instrumental—particularly as it concerned economic matters. Much, perhaps most, of the public policy in American history was enunciated through statute—which quite often was a means of furthering a concept of economic planning (Soule, 1967). That is "public" law; Holmes was talking about "private" law. There is, even now, no adequate theoretical formulation of the place of public law in the American legal system. Our institutions and our theories are largely drawn from feudalistic, prescientific days, a time when public law was relatively nonexistent. Legal theorists have concentrated for the most part on judges and courts and have failed to appreciate the historical importance of legislation and the contemporaneous importance of both legislation and administration.

RELEVANT HYPOTHESES

The exposition below is based on the already-stated proposition that science means change and, further, that the law gives no guarantee that it is adequate to cope with the tensions emanating from a situation in which change, as Warner (1962) has said, "is built into the very nature of [the] social system." A number of hypotheses may be advanced, including the following.

SCIENCE UNDERMINES THE TRADITIONAL JURISTIC ORDER

Law as interdiction is a truly conservative force, and, as such, it resists change; certainly it is accurate to say that law (i.e., legal theory) proceeded in the past by denying change; this was due principally to the fact that most law was private law, and was judge-made. Only in fairly recent times has the instrumental aspect been perceived. Now used to put into official form a wide range of public policies that were spawned by scientific-technological developments, no longer, accordingly, is it possible to think in terms of an *elegantia juris*, of a heaven of internally consistent legal concepts. Rather, it has become necessary to view law as a process of decision taking place as a part of, and as a response to, the total community system, a process that encompasses all organs of public government and many entities of private governance. *In short, law must be viewed as process, rather than as static system*; it is fluid and open-ended, always in a state of becoming. Legal scholars can no longer look backward only, to see where man has been, to deal with the legal problems of the day; the necessity is for purposive thinking or, perhaps better, teleological thinking.

Put another way, we are witnessing the transformation, in Rosinski's (1965) words, of man's way of life "from an 'existence' into an unending 'process.'" The changes wrought by science and technology have produced a public-law explosion. One may deplore or applaud this development; what one cannot do is ignore it. The theoretical foundation of our juristic order has been shattered.

But law *qua* interdiction is not adequate to present-day needs; Frampton (1965) recently said that it "will not arrest a society speeding without presently known theoretical limitations toward denser population, faster transportation and communication, higher mobility, more intricate machinery, faster automatic processing of data and performance of 'mental' operations, and larger size in units of organized religion, education, government, and business." Law, in other words, has been and is being used by legal technicians to aid science and technology as ends in themselves; the humanistic element has not been applied in any significant degree.

SCIENCE UNDERMINES THE TRADITIONAL POLITICAL ORDER

More concretely, scientific change contributes substantially to the growth of pluralistic centers of power—principally the business corporation—which present critical questions of their relationship to the natural person and to the state (Miller, 1968). The nature of government is being transformed. According to some (e.g., Lowi, 1969), our constitutional order is breaking down; it is unable to cope adequately with the pressing needs of the age.

The rise of the giant business corporations provides apt illustration. Because of them and other social groupings, the individualistic base of law no longer exists. Replacing the individual is the group; a person, speaking generally, derives his significance (and psychologically even more than that) by being a member of a group or groups. *Instead of the individual there is a collectivity; the fundamental unit of the political order is now the social group.*

The development may be seen in several areas of law. For a number of years, the Supreme Court, although purportedly speaking in terms of personal freedoms, has been engaged in building a constitutional law of group association (Horn, 1956). In labor law, state encouragement of union organization has helped to construct a system of industrial jurisprudence, derived from interpretations of the statutes and, more importantly, the collective bargaining agreements. Contract law, furthermore, has changed in fact with the rise of "contracts of adhesion" to dominance in the economy. Freedom of contract, the myth to the contrary notwithstanding, has degenerated into the attenuated freedom to choose which agreement one will adhere to (Friedmann, 1959).

Furthermore, science and technology, by contributing to the growth of large business units, have helped to establish a system of private centers of political power—private governments, in other words. The giant corporation is a private government because it: (a) makes decisions of national or social importance; (b) acts in concert with government; (c) acts as an agency of administration for government; and (d) has a political order in its internal operations.

THE STRUCTURE OF GOVERNMENT IS BEING ALTERED BY SCIENCE

Old lines of constitutional demarcation are breaking down under the impact of scientific-technological developments. At least four separate strands of development are visible. First, federalism—all the talk about "creative" or "new" federalism to the contrary—has become moribund as a viable principle of government. A nation with supercorporations and with economic planning (even the minimal American form of planning) can no longer be truly federal. The giant firms and central planning require unified if not uniform policies throughout the nation. The American economy is national, decentralized on a fragmented political order, with the consequence that the states are rapidly becoming anachronisms in the body politic. They are more important as administrative districts for centrally established policies—both public and private—than as separate political units.

Second, the division of powers within the national government is being eroded. Power is flowing toward the Executive. Congress does not have the institutional capacity to deal effectively with the many public policies of the age. It is in the same position as the British Parliament, described by Lord Jackson of Burnley (1967) as in need of finding "a way of getting to grips more effectively with scientific and technological issues"; if it does not, he said, "its functions would be little more than enforcing, on limited information, decisions already taken at ministerial level." As with Congress, so too with the courts: Despite all the furor over the Warren Court, it is not only the least dangerous branch, it is the least powerful.

Third, the nation-state is becoming obsolescent as a form of social order. Public policies tend increasingly to have a larger-than-nation resolution. One of the prime causes of the development—which, stated another way, involves a progressive blurring of the line between what is domestic and what is foreign—is the manner in which

American business has become global—"geo-centric," to use Perlmutter's (1969) label. Slowly but seemingly surely, a sociological community is being buit among the nations along the North Atlantic littoral—the so-called rich man's club. In 1965, *Science* magazine stated flatly: "Technologically, the Atlantic Community exists." So it does—and it may already have its constitution in the treaty establishing the Organization for Economic Cooperation and Development.

Finally, the line—always dimmer than many supposed—between public and private in America is being steadily erased. A convergence of economic and political power may be seen; the label for this is the "techno-corporate state" (Miller, 1968). Seen best in the arms industry, it is even more widespread—and goes beyond business as such to encompass such other groups as farmers (McConnell, 1966). Nieburg (1966), describing the arms producers, said: "Instead of fighting 'creeping socialism,' [American] industry on an enormous scale has become the agent of a fundamentally new economic system which at once resembles traditional private enterprise and the corporate state of fascism."

These fundamental structural changes in government, it should be stressed, are taking place without formal amendment of the Constitution of 1787. The Supreme Court, acting as the *instrument* but not the *cause* of change, has placed its imprimatur on the first, second, and fourth— to the extent that issues concerning them are litigated (which is seldom, de Tocqueville's aphorism about political questions eventually being cast before the Court for decision no longer being valid). Custom and usage, plus some actions of the President and Congress, have contributed substantially to the alterations in the structure of government. Illustrations are numerous, and need not, per William of Occam, be needlessly multiplied, for the point is a truism. Two examples will serve to show what has happened: Despite express constitutional provisions to the contrary, the war-making power is now presidential, and the power of veto over proposed legislation has become legislative.

SCIENCE HAS CONTRIBUTED SUBSTANTIALLY TO THE GROWTH OF THE "ADMINISTRATIVE STATE"

Here, too, special problems are posed for law and the legal system, not the least of which is the apparent fact that much of law has been merged into the political process; it has become "politicized." As said above, the conventional legal wisdom has not adequately met this challenge.

The administrative state means that the United States is basically a nation made up of bureaucracies, both public and private. Their growth, has created a pressing need for means to check them—to insure that humanistic values are served—while simultaneously permitting the tasks of governing the nation to be accomplished (government being an amalgam of both private and public bureaucracies). The high degree of deference that has hitherto been paid to the putative expert—the technological elite—is now being challenged in some quarters. No longer are some Americans willing to remain quiescent while experts contribute substantially to the "deprovement" of life. As a consequence, the legal system—particularly the judiciary—is being increasingly employed by those who dissent. The lawyer's question—"What are your reasons?"—is being asked more and more. New areas of law, in which the expertise of the lawyer can be brought to bear, are opening up, such as in the field of combatting the several types of environmental pollution. A number of lawyers, particularly the relatively young, are vitally interested in taking action beyond the narrow interests of their clients.

The scene, however, is far from being completely affirmative; the tendency just mentioned is more incipient than actual. No doubt most lawyers still are client-bound and income-oriented, with the public interest an empty slogan. There are still few—far too few—Naders and Yannacones—lawyers willing to tackle some of the problems brought by blind adherence to technological progress with little or no regard for the consequences.

The lawyer *qua* social engineer can and should help to plan the future. Helmer (1966) has said that a multitude of possible futures are possible and that *"appropriate* intervention can make a difference in their probabilities." It is in of major assistance to his fellow creatures on this beleaguered planet.

their probabilities." It is in making that "appropriate intervention" that the lawyer could be of major assistance to his fellow creatures on this beleaguered planet.

SCIENCE HAS THE POTENTIAL, AND PROBABLY THE ACTUALITY, OF ADVERSE EFFECTS ON THE HUMAN PERSONALITY

This comes about in such matters as medical experiments on human beings, which have at times been conducted without the knowledge of the patient. Doctors, acting in their conception of the general good, have done this, while lawyers have done little or nothing about it. Science also vastly increases the noise level, permits medication of people without their consent (as in water fluoridation), allows for massive invasion of privacy through dossier technology, and raises the level of radiation in the nation. These examples of scientific "progress" may well be based on false assumptions and a disdain for applying the human equation. Ozbekhan (1967) presents the dimensions of the basic problem: Speaking of dossier technology and the invasion of privacy, he says that

> at the technical level, this confronts us with interesting problems of how to insure privacy and security and how to design the required identification devices that will permit access [to the proposed national data bank] only to those who need to know, and at times and in circumstances when they have to know. However, technical progress has not been spectacular mainly because, in order to solve the technical problem, social norms must first be established and defined. Work leading towards such definition has hardly begun. We do not know what properties of privacy have social value and need to be preserved. We do not know how to sort out with any precision the kind of information to which access must be prohibited. We do not quite understand the complex legal, jurisdictional and, ultimately, constitutional mechanisms that are involved.

To all of this lawyers have been mute, or almost so. Little has been done by government lawyer, practicing lawyer, or academic lawyer to meet the problem posed by Ozbekhan. It *is* lawyers' business, and one could even say that for some—particularly those in Academia—there is a duty and a responsibility to do some *pro bono publico* work of a jurisprudential nature (as well as the nitty-gritty tasks in tackling the nasty everyday problems). We are facing a crisis of critical proportions: The assault on the human psyche has been accelerating for decades; it has now reached a crescendo. Looking around the buzzing, booming confusion of life, one is unable to perceive any group in a better position to do this than the legal "profession." (The word is put in quotes, for it appears obvious that most of the bar in America has been deprofessionalized.) To repeat: We have reached the point where the future must be planned for in a humanistic sense. Our future is being planned for us by the technocrats in business and government. A counterrevolution is necessary.

SCIENCE BOTH EXACERBATES HUMAN PROBLEMS AND GIVES PROMISE OF THEIR REASONABLE RESOLUTION

It makes the human condition worse by such nonserendipitous effects as radiation and pollution, death-control measures that largely cause the population explosion, and by bringing people closer together through transportation and communication. On the other hand, it gives promise that through the use of what Weinberg (1966) calls "technological fixes," some of the appalling social conditions on the planet can be alleviated. One such fix might be an inexpensive means of desalinating water, which might make a considerable difference in the living standards in the Middle East. That would not necessarily eleminate that festering sore in the world scene, but it could not fail to help. Weinberg notes, however, the enormous gap between even the hardest scientific and technological problems and those faced by the social engineer. The latter are infinitely more difficult:

> We technologists shall not satisfy our social engineers, who tell us that our Technological Fixes do not get to the heart of the problem; they are at best temporary expedients; they create new problems as they solve old ones; to put a technological fix into effect requires a positive social action. Eventually, social engineering, like the Supreme Court's decision on desegregation, must be invoked to solve social problems. And of course our social engineers are right. Technology will never *replace* social engineering. But technology was provided and will continue to provide to the social engineer broader options, to make intractable social problems less intractable; perhaps most of all, technology will buy time, that precious commodity that converts violent social revolution into acceptable social evolution.

CONCLUSION

If Weinberg is correct, and I am inclined to agree with him, the opportunity and challenge for lawyers is obvious—and unmet. Scientists and technologists cannot do the job of engineering proper social change. They need help from the one profession that does have some expertise, however minimal, in patching up the wounds of society. Heretofore, law has been used, with the lawyers as willing servants, to further scientific change without regard to consequences; the legal profession has gladly—blindly—helped to make the American commitment to technology "irresistible, irrevocable, and irreversible" (Green, 1967: 12). Legal mechanics or technocrats themselves, they are the products of a system of legal education that prides itself on being nonnormative in orientation. The law schools have failed and the lawyers have failed to meet the challenges of social change brought on by science and technology.

One would indeed have to be a glandular optimist to believe that any significant change will come within the profession. Perhaps it will; noted above have been a few stirrings in a humanistic direction. But if the legal profession does change, legal education will have to become avowedly normative, and law firms will have to become truly professional. A pro bono publico orientation for all segments of the profession is a necessity.

Necessary also is a new way of thinking—prospective or purposive rather than retrospective. Normation must become part of legal education; we must know what we want. Problems must be anticipated and dealt with before they happen. That poor excuse for not having a philosophy—pragmatism—must give way to an open adherence to a set of humanistic values. At no place in the legal system has change kept up with science and technology. But that cannot last, simply because it is absurd—in that it has become clear beyond peradventure that scientific change can no longer be an end in itself.

REFERENCES

BELL, D. (1967) "Notes on the post-industrial state." Public Interest 6 (Winter): 24-35.

BURNLEY, LORD J. (1967) The Times (London). August 31:4.

FRAMPTON, G. (1965) "Scientific Eclat and technological change: some implications for legal education." Michigan Law Rev. 63: 1423.

FRIEDMANN, W. (1959) Law in a Changing Society. Berkeley: Univ. of California Press.

GREEN, H. P. (1967) "The new technological era: a view from the law." Bull. of the Atomic Scientists.

HART, H. L. A. (1961) The Concept of Law. London: Oxford Univ. Press.

HELMER, O. (1966) Social Technology. New York: Basic Books.

HORN. R. (1956) Groups and the Constitution. Stanford: Stanford Univ. Press.

LOWI, T. (1969) The End of Liberalism. New York: W. W. Norton.

MILLER, A. S. (1968) "Toward the techno-corporate state? An essay in American constitutionalism." Villanova Law Rev. 14 (Fall): 1-73.

NAGEL, E. (1961) The Structure of Science: Problems in the Logic of Scientific Explanation. New York: Harcourt, Brace & World.

NIEBURG, H. L. (1966) In the Name of Science. Chicago: Quadrangle.

OZBEKHAN, H. (1967) "Automation." Sci. J. (October): 67.

PERLMUTTER, H. (1969) "Multinational corporations." Columbia J. of World Business (January-February).

ROZINSKI, H. (1965) Power and Human Destiny. New York: Frederick A. Praeger.

SCHON, D. A. (1967) Technology and Change. New York: Delacorte.

SOULE, G. (1967) Planning U.S.A. New York: Viking.

WARNER, W. L. (1962) The Corporation in the Emergent American Society. New York: Harper & Row.

WEINBERG, A. (1966) "Can technology replace social engineering?" Univ. of Chicago Magazine (October): 6.

The Authors

THEODORE L. BECKER is currently a Visiting Professor of Political Science at New York University on leave from the University of Hawaii. He is the author of numerous articles and of *Political Behaviorism and Modern Jurisprudence* (1964, Rand McNally) and *Comparative Judicial Politics* (1970, Rand McNally). He holds a Ph.D. from Northwestern and an LL.B. from Rutgers.

DONALD T. CAMPBELL is a Professor of Psychology at Northwestern University. He is best known for his contributions to social science methodology in the areas of measurement validity and quasi-experimental design.

C. THOMAS DIENES is presently Assistant Professor of Law and Political Science at the University of Houston. He was a Russell Sage Fellow in Law and the Social Sciences at Northwestern University, where he received his law degree and Ph.D. in political science. He has published articles dealing with legal policy change in the areas of birth control, artificial insemination, and welfare law and serves as consultant to a number of poverty organizations.

YEHEZKEL DROR is currently a Senior Staff Member of The RAND Corporation in Santa Monica, California. He is on leave from the Hebrew University of Jerusalem, where he recently was the Chairman of the Political Science Department. He authored *Public Policymaking Reexamined*, and his main interest is policy sciences.

GENE V GLASS is Associate Professor and staff member of the Laboratory of Educational Research at the University of Colorado in Boulder, Colorado. His research specializations are statistics, experimental design, and evaluation. His most important recent publication is *Statistical Methods in Education and Psychology* (1970), a textbook written with Dr. Julian C. Stanley of The Johns Hopkins University.

JOEL B. GROSSMAN is Associate Professor of Political Science at the University of Wisconsin, where he has taught since 1963. He is also Associate Director of the Center for Law and Behavioral Science at Wisconsin, and is the author of *Lawyers and Judges* (1965), coeditor of *Frontiers of Judicial Research* (1969), and author of numerous articles in professional journals.

JOHN N. HAZARD has been a Professor of Public Law at Columbia University since 1946 and was the advisor on Soviet Law to the United States prosecutor in the preparation of the Nuremberg indictment in 1945. He is currently serving as President of the International Association of Legal Science, and is the author of several books, including *Communists and their Law,* and *The Soviet System of Government.*

C. RAY JEFFERY is presently a Professor of Public Administration at New York University, and in the fall of 1970 he will be a member of the faculty at Florida State University, in the Department of Criminology and Corrections. He has been Book Review Editor for the *Journal of Criminal Law, Criminology, and Police Science,* and is currently editor of *Criminologica.*

JAMES P. LEVINE is an Assistant Professor of Political Science at the University of Oregon. Before coming to Oregon he served in the same capacity at Michigan State University. Currently his research interests include civil liberties, conditioning of police, and the impact of the Supreme Court.

ARTHUR SELWYN MILLER is presently Professor of Law at the George Washington University. He is the author of numerous articles in both legal and nonlegal periodicals, and of the books *Racial Discrimination and Private Education* (1957), *The Supreme Court and American Capitalism* (1968), and *The Supreme Court and the Living Constitution* (1969).

STUART S. NAGEL is a Professor of Political Science at the University of Illinois. He has been a Fellow of the Center for Advanced Study in the Behavioral Sciences and an Attorney to the Office of Economic Opportunity. He is the author of *The Legal Process from a Behavioral Perspective* (1969, Dorsey) and is currently working on a book entitled *Effects of Alternative Legal Policies.*

H. LAURENCE ROSS is a Professor of Sociology and Law at the University of Denver, and is currently on leave as Fulbright Lecturer at the University of Louvain in Belgium. He was previously Chairman of the Department of Sociology at University College, New York University, and spent a year as Staff Behavioral Scientist at the Northwestern University Traffic Institute. His publications include *Settled Out of Court,* (Aldine, 1970); *Crimes Against Bureaucracy* (edited with Erwin O. Smigel, Van Nostrand, 1970); and *Perspectives on the Social Order,* (McGraw-Hill, 1963 and 1968).

Date Due